Layers of Learning

Year One • Unit Thirteen

Ancient India
Grasslands
Elements
Texture & Form

HooDoo Publishing
United States of America
©2014 Layers of Learning
Copies of maps or activities may be made for a particular family or classroom.
ISBN 978-1494983291

If you wish to reproduce or print excerpts of this publication, please contact us at contact@layers-of-learning.com for permission. Thank you for respecting copyright laws.

Units At A Glance: Topics For All Four Years of the Layers of Learning Program

1	History	Geography	Science	The Arts
1	Mesopotamia	Maps & Globes	Planets	Cave Paintings
2	Egypt	Map Keys	Stars	Egyptian Art
3	Europe	Global Grids	Earth & Moon	Crafts
4	Ancient Greece	Wonders	Satellites	Greek Art
5	Babylon	Mapping People	Humans in Space	Poetry
6	The Levant	Physical Earth	Laws of Motion	List Poems
7	Phoenicians	Oceans	Motion	Moral Stories
8	Assyrians	Deserts	Fluids	Rhythm
9	Persians	Arctic	Waves	Melody
10	Ancient China	Forests	Machines	Chinese Art
11	Early Japan	Mountains	States of Matter	Line & Shape
12	Arabia	Rivers & Lakes	Atoms	Color & Value
13	Ancient India	Grasslands	Elements	Texture & Form
14	Ancient Africa	Africa	Bonding	African Tales
15	First North Americans	North America	Salts	Creative Kids
16	Ancient South America	South America	Plants	South American Art
17	Celts	Europe	Flowering Plants	Jewelry
18	Roman Republic	Asia	Trees	Roman Art
19	Christianity	Australia & Oceania	Simple Plants	Instruments
20	Roman Empire	You Explore	Fungi	Composing Music

2	History	Geography	Science	The Arts
1	Byzantines	Turkey	Climate & Seasons	Byzantine Art
2	Barbarians	Ireland	Forecasting	Illumination
3	Islam	Arabian Peninsula	Clouds & Precipitation	Creative Kids
4	Vikings	Norway	Special Effects	Viking Art
5	Anglo Saxons	Britain	Wild Weather	King Arthur Tales
6	Charlemagne	France	Cells and DNA	Carolingian Art
7	Normans	Nigeria	Skeletons	Canterbury Tales
8	Feudal System	Germany	Muscles, Skin, & Cardiopulmonary	Gothic Art
9	Crusades	Balkans	Digestive & Senses	Religious Art
10	Burgundy, Venice, Spain	Switzerland	Nerves	Oil Paints
11	Wars of the Roses	Russia	Health	Minstrels & Plays
12	Eastern Europe	Hungary	Metals	Printmaking
13	African Kingdoms	Mali	Carbon Chem	Textiles
14	Asian Kingdoms	Southeast Asia	Non-metals	Vivid Language
15	Mongols	Caucasus	Gases	Fun With Poetry
16	Medieval China & Japan	China	Electricity	Asian Arts
17	Pacific Peoples	Micronesia	Circuits	Arts of the Islands
18	American Peoples	Canada	Technology	Indian Legends
19	The Renaissance	Italy	Magnetism	Renaissance Art I
20	Explorers	Caribbean Sea	Motors	Renaissance Art II

3	History	Geography	Science	The Arts
1	Age of Exploration	Argentina and Chile	Classification & Insects	Fairy Tales
2	The Ottoman Empire	Egypt and Libya	Reptiles & Amphibians	Poetry
3	Mogul Empire	Pakistan & Afghanistan	Fish	Mogul Arts
4	Reformation	Angola & Zambia	Birds	Reformation Art
5	Renaissance England	Tanzania & Kenya	Mammals & Primates	Shakespeare
6	Thirty Years' War	Spain	Sound	Baroque Music
7	The Dutch	Netherlands	Light & Optics	Baroque Art I
8	France	Indonesia	Bending Light	Baroque Art II
9	The Enlightenment	Korean Pen.	Color	Art Journaling
10	Russia & Prussia	Central Asia	History of Science	Watercolors
11	Conquistadors	Baltic States	Igneous Rocks	Creative Kids
12	Settlers	Peru & Bolivia	Sedimentary Rocks	Native American Art
13	13 Colonies	Central America	Metamorphic Rocks	Settler Sayings
14	Slave Trade	Brazil	Gems & Minerals	Colonial Art
15	The South Pacific	Australasia	Fossils	Principles of Art
16	The British in India	India	Chemical Reactions	Classical Music
17	Boston Tea Party	Japan	Reversible Reactions	Folk Music
18	Founding Fathers	Iran	Compounds & Solutions	Rococo
19	Declaring Independence	Samoa and Tonga	Oxidation & Reduction	Creative Crafts I
20	The American Revolution	South Africa	Acids & Bases	Creative Crafts II

4	History	Geography	Science	The Arts
1	American Government	USA	Heat & Temperature	Patriotic Music
2	Expanding Nation	Pacific States	Motors & Engines	Tall Tales
3	Industrial Revolution	U.S. Landscapes	Energy	Romantic Art I
4	Revolutions	Mountain West States	Energy Sources	Romantic Art II
5	Africa	U.S. Political Maps	Energy Conversion	Impressionism I
6	The West	Southwest States	Earth Structure	Impressionism II
7	Civil War	National Parks	Plate Tectonics	Post-Impressionism
8	World War I	Plains States	Earthquakes	Expressionism
9	Totalitarianism	U.S. Economics	Volcanoes	Abstract Art
10	Great Depression	Heartland States	Mountain Building	Kinds of Art
11	World War II	Symbols and Landmarks	Chemistry of Air & Water	War Art
12	Modern East Asia	The South States	Food Chemistry	Modern Art
13	India's Independence	People of America	Industry	Pop Art
14	Israel	Appalachian States	Chemistry of Farming	Modern Music
15	Cold War	U.S. Territories	Chemistry of Medicine	Free Verse
16	Vietnam War	Atlantic States	Food Chains	Photography
17	Latin America	New England States	Animal Groups	Latin American Art
18	Civil Rights	Home State Study	Instincts	Theater & Film
19	Technology	Home State Study II	Habitats	Architecture
20	Terrorism	America in Review	Conservation	Creative Kids

Unit 1-13 Printable Pack

This unit includes printables at the end. To make life easier for you we also created digital printable packs for each unit. To retrieve your printable pack for Unit 1-13, please visit

www.layers-of-learning.com/digital-printable-packs/

Put the printable pack in your shopping cart and use this coupon code:

0111UNIT1-13

Your printable pack will be free.

LAYERS OF LEARNING INTRODUCTION

This is part of a series of units in the Layers of Learning homeschool curriculum, including the subjects of history, geography, science, and the arts. Children from 1st through 12th can participate in the same curriculum at the same time - family school style.

The units are intended to be used in order as the basis of a complete curriculum (once you add in a systematic math, reading, and writing program). You begin with Year 1 Unit 1 no matter what ages your children are. Spend about 2 weeks on each unit. You pick and choose the activities within the unit that appeal to you and read the books from the book list that are available to you or find others on the same topic from your library. We highly recommend that you use the timeline in every history section as the backbone. Then flesh out your learning with reading and activities that highlight the topics you think are the most important.

Alternatively, you can use the units as activity ideas to supplement another curriculum in any order you wish. You can still use them with all ages of children at the same time.

When you've finished with Year One, move on to Year Two, Year Three, and Year Four. Then begin again with Year One and work your way through the years again. Now your children will be older, reading more involved books, and writing more in depth. When you have completed the sequence for the second time, you start again on it for the third and final time. If your student began with Layers of Learning in 1st grade and stayed with it all the way through she would go through the four year rotation three times, firmly cementing the information in her mind in ever increasing depth. At each level you should expect increasing amounts of outside reading and writing. High schoolers in particular should be reading extensively, and if possible, participating in discussion groups.

☺ ☺ ☺ These icons will guide you in spotting activities and books that are appropriate for the age of child you are working with. But if you think an activity is too juvenile or too difficult for your kids, adjust accordingly. The icons are not there as rules, just guides.

☺ GRADES 1-4
☺ GRADES 5-8
☺ GRADES 9-12

Within each unit we share:
- EXPLORATIONS, activities relating to the topic;
- EXPERIMENTS, usually associated with science topics;
- EXPEDITIONS, field trips;
- EXPLANATIONS, teacher helps or educational philosophies.

In the sidebars we also include Additional Layers, Famous Folks, Fabulous Facts, On the Web, and other extra related topics that can take you off on tangents, exploring the world and your interests with a bit more freedom. The curriculum will always be there to pull you back on track when you're ready.

You can learn more about how to use this curriculum at www.layers-of-learning.com/layers-of-learning-program/

ANCIENT INDIA – GRASSLANDS – ELEMENTS – TEXTURE & FORM

UNIT THIRTEEN
ANCIENT INDIA – GRASSLANDS – ELEMENTS – TEXTURE & FORM

The first duty of man is the seeking after and the investigation of truth.
-Cicero, Roman Statesman

LIBRARY LIST:

HISTORY

Search for: Ancient India, Buddha, Buddhism
- ☺ Rama and the Demon King by Jessica Souhami. A tale from the Ramayana, the ancient holy book of India, in a picture book format.
- ☺ Indian Children's Favourite Stories by Rosemarie Somaiah and Ranjan Somaiah. Traditional stories from India.
- ☺ The Little Book of Hindu Deities: From the Goddess of Wealth to the Sacred Cow by Sanjay Patel. Great introduction to Hindu mythology with fun illustrations.
- ☺ ☺ Life in the Ancient Indus River Valley by Hazel Richardson. Fact filled and image filled, explains difficult concepts like Nirvana, for kids.
- ☺ ☺ Ramayana: Divine Loophole by Sanjay Patel. 186 page picture book that will appeal to kids from five to fifteen. Follows the adventures of Rama and his quest to rescue his wife after the demon king kidnaps her. The author/illustrator is a Pixar animator.
- ☺ Buddhism by Philip Wilkinson. For ages 9-12.
- ☺ Eyewitness: India by Manini Chatterjee and Anita Roy. For ages 9-12.
- ☺ The Ramayana for Young Readers by Milly Acharya. For ages 9-12.
- ☺ Prince of Ayodhya by Ashok K. Banker. This is book one of the Ramayana series. Masterfully written, this fictionalized re-telling of the Ramayana will give readers insight into ancient Indian myths and culture.
- ☺ Siddhartha. For high school and above, tells the story of the Buddha and his quest for enlightenment

GEOGRAPHY

Search for: grasslands, steppes, plains, savannah, pampas
- ☺ Grasslands: Fields of Green and Gold by Laura Purdi Salas.
- ☺ If You're Not From the Prairie by David Bouchard. Poetically explains why howling winds, blistering heat, and an endless sky win the devotion of those who live with them.
- ☺ ☺ Explore the Grasslands by Kay Jackson. Part of a well-written series on biomes.
- ☺ ☺ A Walk in the Prairie by Rebecca L. Johnson.
- ☺ ☺ ☺ Draw Grassland Animals by Doug Dubosque. A step-by-step how to draw book.

ANCIENT INDIA – GRASSLANDS – ELEMENTS – TEXTURE & FORM

SCIENCE

Search for: periodic table, elements

☻ ☻ ☻ The Elements: A Visual Exploration of Every Known Atom in the Universe by Theodore Gray and Nick Mann. Includes photographs and descriptions of every element in the order they appear on the periodic table.

☻ The Periodic Table: Elements with Style! By Simon Basher and Adrian Dingle. Elements presented in a fun and memorable way.

☻ ☻ Periodic Tales: A Cultural History of the Elements, from Arsenic to Zinc by Hugh Aldersey-Williams. Takes you through the elements one by one, relating anecdotes and culturally interesting information about each one. It's definitely not a heavy science intensive book, but more a way to become comfortable and familiar with the elements and what role they actually play in your everyday life.

☻ ☻ The Mystery of the Periodic Table by Benjamin Wiker and Jeanne Bendick. Brings you through the historical journey of our discovery of the elements and the periodic table, explaining the elements as you move along.

☻ The Periodic Table: Its Story and Its Significance by Eric R. Scerri. Takes the reader through the history and development of the current periodic table, refreshingly covering all the wrong turns and dead ends along the way as well as discussion of what we still do not know.

☻ The Disappearing Spoon by Sam Klein. Full of history and anecdotes centering around the periodic table. Tales of war, towering egos, and laboratory pranks.

THE ARTS

Search for: texture in art, art texture, Van Gogh, and picture books illustrated by Garth Williams, Maurice Sendak, the D'Aulaire's, or Robert Lawson (to show examples of texture in art.)

☻ What is Texture? By Stephanie Fitzgerald.

☻ Vincent Van Gogh: Sunflowers and Swirly Stars by Joan Holub. Written as a child's report about Van Gogh, this book contains tons of interesting tidbits about the artist alongside reproductions of some of his art.

☻ Vincent's Colors from the Metropolitan Museum of Art. Uses the author's loosely translated words as a simple accompaniment to his paintings.

☻ ☻ Making Amazing Art: 40 Activities Using the 7 Elements of Art Design by Sandi Henry. To take your study of art techniques further with fun projects to try.

☻ ☻ What Makes A Van Gogh A Van Gogh? By Richard Muhlberger. Goes into detail about the techniques used by Van Gogh that set his style apart from others.

☻ Vincent Van Gogh: Portrait of an Artist by Jan Greenberg and Sandra Jordan. Biography of Van Gogh that draws on letters written between the artist and his brother. Includes Van Gogh's struggles with mental illness and discusses his suicide.

☻ ☻ Van Gogh: Explore Vincent Van Gogh's Life and Art, and the Influences That Shaped His Work by Bruce Bernard. From DK, this book is visually stunning, packed with little tidbits about both Van Gogh's life and his paintings.

☻ Texture and Detail in Watercolor by Richard Bolton. For the advanced art student.

ANCIENT INDIA – GRASSLANDS – ELEMENTS – TEXTURE & FORM

HISTORY: ANCIENT INDIA

Fabulous Fact

Ancient Indians hunted, practiced martial arts, fenced, and wrestled.

Additional Layer

The Indus Valley civilizations were probably the earliest to develop standard weights and measures. Why is it important to have standards in lengths and weights? What if we didn't know an inch is an inch or a gram is a gram? How would that change how we buy shoes or peanut butter or travel to Grandma's house?

Fabulous Fact

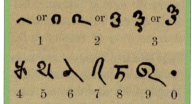

Ancient India gave us our current number system – nine digits, the zero, and the decimal.

Archaeologists have found copious amounts of written records from the Indus Valley dating back to ancient times in India. Unfortunately, no one has yet learned to read these ancient Dravidian writings and so we know very little about the people of this time and place. Later the Vedic speaking peoples invaded and we *can* read their writings.

Even though we can't read their writings we know the most ancient people of the Indus Valley were a highly developed, complex society. They had writings; they had carefully planned cities with straight streets and sewage systems; they made beautiful art and traded all over the known world. They also stored food in granaries, invented the use of cotton for cloth, and had large public bathhouses in every city.

Their way of life came to an end when the Aryans invaded in 1500 BC. The Aryans became the new ruling and religious class, and just to make sure everyone knew their place, they introduced caste systems. The Aryans could not write so their religion, stories, and history were passed down by word of mouth for hundreds of years before they were written down in 1000 BC. This book became known as the Rigveda, which is a history and religious volume in one.

This is a scene of the frame story, a snake sacrifice, where King Janamejaya tells the epic of the Mahabharata.

☺ ☺ ☻ **EXPLORATION: Ancient Indian Timeline**
You will find printable timeline squares at the end of this unit.
- c. 3500 BC Farmers settle in the Indus valley
- 3120 BC Mythical war of the Mahabharata
- c. 2500-1800 BC Indus valley civilization at its height
- c. 1500 BC Aryan tribes from the northwest invade

ANCIENT INDIA – GRASSLANDS – ELEMENTS – TEXTURE & FORM

- 1000 BC The Rigveda are composed
- 876 BC Hindus invent the concept of zero
- 700 BC Caste system begun
- c. 560-480 BC Siddhartha Gautama (Buddha) lives
- 500 BC Jainism developed in Northern India
- 321 BC The Mauryan Empire begins
- 272-231 BC Ashoka the Great is emperor
- 250 BC First Buddhist cave temples are carved
- 185 BC Mauryan Empire collapses
- 100 BC India is divided into many states, the most powerful being Bactria (northwest) and Sunga (east)
- 100 BC The Bhagavad Gita is composed
- 50 AD Thomas, the apostle of Jesus, visits India
- 320-535 AD Gupta Empire
- c. 495 Huns invade northern India
- c. 550-1206 AD Dozens of small states vie for power in India
- 1206-1526 Delhi Sultanate rules a large portion of India

☺ ☻ **EXPLORATION: Harrapa and Mohenjo-Daro**
Harrapa and Mohenjo-Daro were two ancient Indian cities in the Indus Valley, the remains of which were discovered in 1922. Hundreds more cities and settlements have been found since that time in the same region, and we collectively call them the Indus Valley Civilization. They existed at the same time the Egyptians and Sumerians lived anciently.

We know quite a bit about their lives from the things that were discovered there. They lived in two story mud brick homes with courtyards. Their homes had wells and even sewer lines for indoor plumbing. The people wore colorful robes and jewelry, danced, played with toys, and ate things like bread, rice, fruits, vegetables, fish, pork, and other meats. Their buildings were well-built and beautiful, their cities perfectly organized with square blocks and

Mohenjo-Daro Ruins

Additional Layer

The ancient Indians had pets. The most common pets they kept were exotic birds like parrots and peacocks.

Painting by Archibald Thorburn

There were monkeys all over the place too, but they didn't usually keep them as pets because they were considered such a nuisance.

Additional Layer

Learn more about one of the religions begun in India: Hinduism, Jainism, Buddhism, or Sikhism.

Jain Universe

Ancient India – Grasslands – Elements – Texture & Form

Additional Layer
The geography of the Indus River Valley is similar to the geography of the Nile River Valley and the Fertile Crescent. That is, a rich fertile area of farmland immediately around a river with desert and the sea coast surrounding.

Before partition in 1947, the Indus Valley was entirely in India. Today most of the area is now in Pakistan.

Fabulous Fact

Ancient India, before 1500 BC, is one of the few civilizations on Earth to be free of slavery. It wasn't until the Indo-European invasions that the caste system was introduced.

streets, and their homes all with access to important amenities like water, a sewer system and garbage collection. They were quite advanced.

Make a list of the ways that the Indus River Civilization was like ours today. How were they different?

☺ ☻ ☻ EXPLORATION: Mahajanapadas
After the Indus Valley civilizations there was a period of time known as the Mahajanapadas, sixteen powerful and separate kingdoms and republics. There were many other smaller kingdoms in India at this time as well. However, these larger states were important enough to become part of the Indian Buddhist epics.

These sixteen states and other smaller ones arose from wandering tribes who settled down and created cities. Each kingdom is named after the tribe who settled it. The root word is "janapandas," which means *foothold of a tribe*.

ANCIENT INDIA – GRASSLANDS – ELEMENTS – TEXTURE & FORM

Make a map of these sixteen states using the India map and the state labels worksheet at the end of the unit. Cut out the names of each state and glue it onto the map in the correct spot. Use the pictured map for reference.

☺ ☺ ☺ **EXPLORATION: Mauryan Empire Map**

The Mauryan Empire was the first to unite large areas of India. Before this there were dozens of independent small states. Color a map showing the earliest civilizations around the Indus Valley and then the later Mauryan Empire. Use the Mauryan Empire map from the end of this unit.

Label the Indus Valley and the Mauryan Empire. Color the two areas.

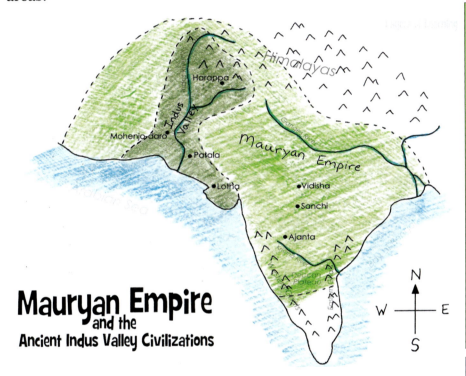

☺ ☺ **EXPLORATION: Indian Dress**

Dress like an Indian. For either boys or girls, get a long piece of cotton cloth. Boys usually wore white and may have worn turbans. Among women, only widows in mourning wore white. Girls wore saris in different ways depending on what they were doing. For working they wore their saris as pants that wrapped up and around their waists and upper bodies. For dressing up they wore their sari like a skirt and then wrapped it up and over one shoulder.

When at war (yes, the women fought in battle too) they wore their sari like pants and kept the top just covering the chest, but not

---

Memorization Station

Empires of Ancient India:

- Indus Valley
- Janapadas
- Maruyan
- Bactria
- Sungas
- Andhras
- Gupta

Teaching Tip

When starting a new history unit, begin with a timeline. You can do timelines individually or as a group on a large wall timeline. Make sure you relate the current topic to other topics you have covered. For Ancient India you would explain that the oldest Indian civilizations were around at the same time as ancient Egypt and Sumeria, the oldest civilizations that we know about.

Fabulous Fact

The Rigveda (composed between 1700 and 1100 BC) is the Hindu scripture, a series of hymns and prayers including a story of the origin of the earth. The Vedic period of India is named after the Rigveda and denotes the time when the Hindu scripture was composed.

Ancient India – Grasslands – Elements – Texture & Form

Additional Layer
The swastika is an ancient Indian symbol, going back as far as the ancient Indus Valley civilizations. The Hindus, Buddhists, and Jains adopted it as their symbol. The symbol has been found on ancient pottery in Greece and Rome and also in China. To the ancients and to modern Buddhists, Hindus, and Jains it symbolizes good luck or well-being.

Unfortunately the Nazis used the swastika and wrecked it by making it symbolize evil totalitarian regimes and white supremacy. Jerks.

Additional Layer
Some people see vegetarianism in a religious or moral context, while others see it as a health issue only.

Does your moral or religious code include any guidelines or rules about food? Most religions do include a health code of some kind.

over the shoulder, to keep their arms free. Indian women sometimes wore a spot of red on their forehead between their eyes as a decoration.

Boys would wrap their cloth around their upper legs and waist to make a sort of pants. These are called a dhoti. A sari is a 5 meter long piece of cloth that is considered one size fits all. Girls can choose any of the styles above to wrap their saris.

On You Tube you can find tutorials to teach you how to put on a sari or a dhoti.

EXPLORATION: Games, Then and Now
Playing cards, chess, and snakes and ladders all originated in ancient India. Play a modern version of these games and explain their origins.

EXPLORATION: Where's The Beef?
Modern Indians are often vegetarians or eat very little meat, but anciently this was not so. They ate wheat, pork, rice, chicken, beef, mutton, and goats. Over time the various religious traditions of India made cows (Hindu), pork (Muslim), and animal sacrifices in general (Hindu) taboo for eating. Try this recipe from India that has been passed down from ancient times.

Chapatis (Indian Flat Bread):
    2 c. whole wheat flour (or mix half white and half wheat)
    ¾ c. water (or milk or yogurt for super smooth bread)
    2 Tbsp. cooking oil
    1 tsp. salt

Mix flour and salt in a bowl. Add oil and water slowly, mixing as you go. Knead the dough thoroughly. Divide the dough into 12 equal portions. Flatten each portion out into a circle using your hands on a floured surface. Fry in a medium hot griddle, flipping halfway.

Served with Indian Curry:
    1 onion, diced
    1 Tbsp. oil
    2 Tbsp. curry powder (The more you add the hotter it gets.
        If your kids aren't used to curry, start out lighter)
    1 tsp. cinnamon

Ancient India – Grasslands – Elements – Texture & Form

1 tsp. paprika
1 tsp. garlic powder
1 Tbsp. tomato paste
1 cup plain yogurt
¾ cup coconut milk
2 cups of either chopped up chicken or vegetables

Saute the onion in the oil; add the chicken, veggies and spices; then saute until cooked through. Then add the yogurt, tomato paste, and coconut milk and cook until it is heated through.

☺ ● EXPLORATION: Elephant Tag

When Alexander the Great died, one of his friends, Seleucius, became the king of some of the eastern provinces (what is now Afghanistan, Iran, Iraq, Syria, and Lebanon, along with parts of several other neighboring countries). War elephants were used by several ancient peoples, including the Seleucids in India. Seleucius not only used war elephants, but also ended up surrendering to Chandra Gupta, an opponent who gifted him 500 war elephants in exchange for not being attacked. Chandra Gupta's army was stronger anyway, and likely would have won regardless. Chandra Gupta wasn't so dumb though—his wise adviser, Kautilya, advised him to gift his oldest elephants. Within 20 years Seleucius had only one elephant left even though elephants live to be around 80 years old.

Elephants had their benefits and their drawbacks in an army. They are big and strong, but not so fast. They can only walk about 2-4 miles per hour. They aren't necessarily agile, maneuverable, or sure-footed when it comes to rough terrain. However, they are quite intimidating, especially in large numbers and fully dressed in war armor. They are sometimes considered to be like an ancient tank, but unlike tanks, they could not be mass-produced and had to be trained.

Fabulous Fact
Even though India is the birthplace of Buddhism, not many Indians are Buddhists today. Instead Buddhism traveled east to China and Southeast Asia where it found its home.

Fabulous Fact
The ancient Indian religions we know about were started after the Indo-Europeans migrated to India from the land around the Black and Caspian Seas. All of the great Indian epics, the Rigveda and the Mahabharata, were written after this invasion. The more ancient people of Mohenjo-daro and Harapa likely had religious beliefs and gods as well, but we know nothing of them.

Writer's Workshop
Siddhartha (see pg. 13) saw things when he went outside the palace that shocked him. He saw a sick and dying man, a person who had just lost a loved one, and even a corpse. Have you ever seen anything that shocked you and made you change the way you think about things forever? Write about it in your writer's notebook.

Ancient India – Grasslands – Elements – Texture & Form

Additional Layers

Siddhartha's dad wanted to protect him and shelter his son from evils and sadness in the world. Was he right to do so? Should parents shelter their children? Do your parents try to protect you from things?

Siddhartha saw a holy man who inspired him to search for more meaning in life. Is there someone who inspires you? What is it about them that strikes you?

Additional Layer

Starting way back with the Mauryan emperors, India has a long history of non-violence, if not always in practice, at least in philosophy. This tradition culminated in the twentieth century with Gandhi, who used non-violent means to free the Indian people from British rule and with Martin Luther King Jr. who used non-violence to free his people in America from crippling discrimination.

Writer's Workshop

Pretend you are Siddhartha and write a letter to your father telling him why you are leaving the palace and going on your quest.

Play Elephant tag by having two people be the elephant (one person riding piggyback). The elephant must tag the other players who are foot soldiers, to get them out. The war elephants were strong, but not necessarily fast. The foot soldiers are quicker, but if the elephant catches them they are out of the game for good – dead on the battlefield.

☺ ☺ ☺ EXPLORATION: Otherwise Known As Buddha

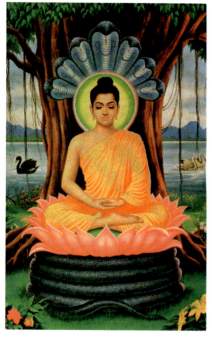

One night, a queen had a dream that a white elephant tore through her body. A short time later, her son, Siddhartha Gautama, was born. The queen was told that her dream meant her son would be either a great ruler or a holy man. He was a prince in India, both wealthy and well-loved. His father wanted him to follow along in his footsteps and become a great king, so he ordered that his son be kept within the palace and taught to be like him, kept free from thinking, meditation, and religion. He was to be kept from seeing anything sad that might make him consider the meaning of life. A part of him always wanted to see what lay beyond the palace walls, so he asked a charioteer to take him away from the palace. Immediately, he was saddened and troubled to see how much suffering and sorrow there was in the world. Having lived such a sheltered and fortunate life, he felt shocked at the pain of the world. He left his home, his wife, and his baby son at age twenty-nine on a quest for enlightenment. He became a monk and traveled around India looking for answers. He studied and listened to a great many teachings, but he finally found his answers all on his own through meditation while sitting under a fig tree, and ever since he was known as "the awakened one," Buddha. He meditated on and taught that life's suffering comes because of our selfish wants. If we stop wanting, we can find peace. He traveled around India and taught for the rest of his life. His proverbs and teachings have now spread and blossomed into one of the world's major religions, with followers all over the globe.

Re-tell the story of Buddha's enlightenment using words and illustrations you've made and color the picture from the printables section at the end of the unit.

ANCIENT INDIA – GRASSLANDS – ELEMENTS – TEXTURE & FORM

😊 😊 😊 EXPEDITION: A Buddhist Temple Near You

Most cities have a Buddhist Temple if you are looking for one to visit. You could go just to see what it looks like on the outside, or make arrangements for a look inside as well. Generally they welcome anyone with interest as long as you are polite and respectful. You may even go and participate in a class or meditation session if you'd like.

Here are a few things done at Buddhist Temples that you can expect:

- Prostration – This is just a term for bowing. When people are in front of a statue of Buddha they bow out of respect.
- Chanting – Expect to hear chanting and the ring of a gong. The chants are the teachings of Buddha and the gongs are meant to announce the meeting time or new parts of the meeting, and also to aid in meditation.
- Lighting incense – This is a way to pay respect to Buddha.
- Altar Offerings – You will likely see offerings of flowers, fruits, and vegetarian dishes at the altar. Since Buddhists don't believe in killing animals for food, you won't see any meat offerings.
- Meditation is a way to purify the mind and body.

A Buddhist Temple in Thailand, photographed by Bill Justus.

😊 😊 😊 EXPLORATION: Cast into a Caste

The caste system in India was made up of 5 different classes of people, all with varying treatment depending upon their social status. The first caste was made up of the Brahmins, who were the priests and holy men. They were the spiritual leaders and were given the utmost respect. The second class was made up of warriors and rulers called kshatriyas. They had a lot of decision making power, but could certainly be overruled by the Brahmins. The third class were the vaisyas, the laborers who were skilled. The unskilled laborers made up the fourth class, the sudras. And finally, the fifth and final class were the pariahs. These people

Famous Folks

Ashoka the Great of the Mauryan Empire conquered most of India through conquest. After witnessing the carnage after a battle he initiated, he felt great remorse and lived the rest of his life as a philanthropic ruler, embracing Buddhism, non-violence, love, and tolerance. Ashoka was instrumental in spreading Buddhism to the rest of Asia.

Additional Layer

Stupas, religious mounds of earth containing relics of the Buddha himself, can be found all over India and other parts of the Buddhist world. Originally stupas were just simple earth mounds, but over time they became more elaborate.

Ancient India – Grasslands – Elements – Texture & Form

Fabulous Fact
Buddhism and Jainism were both religious and social responses to the excesses and worldliness of the powerful Brahmin caste during the sixth century BC.

Additional Layer
People tend to want to have power over others, especially economic power. The caste system was a method used in India to keep certain groups in power. What other methods have been used around the world and at different times in history?

Famous Folks
Chandragupta II the Great was the greatest of the Gupta emperors. It was under his leadership that the greatest flowering of art and knowledge in India took place.

The story of his path to the crown is filled with evil villains, daring rescues, and true love.

His other name is Vikramaditya, a famous name in India, reaching epic proportions.

were responsible for doing the really terrible jobs like burying the dead. They were considered to be filthy, the untouchables, or outcasts in society.

Use the printable at the end of this unit to study the names of each caste according to their place in society. You may want to draw a picture or write a short description of each caste and who the members of it were.

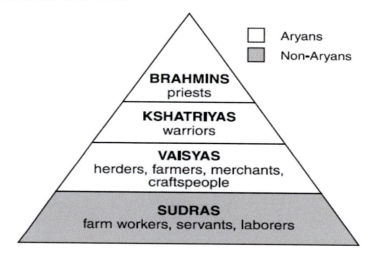

☺ ☺ ☺ **EXPLORATION: The Gupta Empire**
The Gupta Empire existed around the same time as the Roman Empire, and was the golden age of India. The Guptas ruled by keeping conquered kings on their thrones as vassals, subject to the laws of the Guptas and kept in check mainly through diplomacy and marital alliances.

Terracotta art from the Gupta Period

Ancient India – Grasslands – Elements – Texture & Form

The people under the Guptas were free – they could worship as they chose and they were compensated for working. Even writers, artists, and scholars were given money for their creative contributions to society, a rare circumstance in the ancient world. The long period of peace during the Gupta reign from 300 AD to 550 AD meant that prosperity and scholarship, art and music flourished. This is the period when Indians developed the concept of zero as a place holder, invented algebra and postulates in trigonometry, predicted that the earth revolves around the sun, studied eclipses, developed the game of chess, recorded the great Indian epics, and wrote great poetry and plays, all of which influenced the rest of the world down to the modern day.

Each village had protection as well. They were each assigned one squad to protect them from bandits or anyone who might disturb the peace. A squad was made up of an elephant, a chariot, 3 men on horseback, and 5 soldiers. Criminals who were caught had to pay fines for their crimes, but there were no jails and no capital punishment. If a war broke out, the squads were removed from their assigned villages and brought together to form the royal army to defend the empire.

The Gupta Empire fell when the Huns invaded in the sixth century AD. The Huns broke up the empire and left northern India weakened. The aftermath was a couple dozen or so small, weak states, thrown back into a dark age.

Read more about the Gupta Empire online and from the library. Write a simulated journal entry. Pretend that you are a villager who has had their home ransacked. Describe what happens as the squad comes to keep the peace and catch the thief.

Famous Folks

The nine gems were a group of nine scholars who worked in Chandragupta II's court. They were poets, mathematicians, philosophers and artists.

Their names were:
Kalidasa
Vetala Bhatta
Varahamihira
Vararuchi
Amarasimha
Dhanvantari
Bhaktamara Stotra
Shanku
Ghatakarpura

Additional Layer

Interestingly, the Huns were demolishing Europe, the Middle East, and China at the same time as India. Busy guys.

Additional Layer

The Gupta military relied heavily on archers. Their bows were made of steel, if you were a rich noble, or bamboo, if you were rank and file. The longbow of India is massively powerful and shot either steel arrows or bamboo arrows with a steel tip. These missiles could pierce thick armor and take down a war elephant.

GEOGRAPHY: GRASSLANDS

Grasslands are areas where the primary vegetation is made up of grasses. There is not enough water in these areas to support many trees, but it's also not so dry that it becomes a desert. Grasslands can also be created or maintained by human and animal agency. People cut down trees or burn swaths of forest and then prevent new trees from growing by farming the land or grazing animals on it. Grasslands are also naturally maintained by natural fires and grazing of wild herds of bison, buffalo, deer, antelope, and other herbivores in various parts of the world.

Oglala National Grassland, Nebraska, USA

Grasslands have different names depending on the area of the world you live in. In North America they are called plains; in South America, pampas; in Africa savannah or veld; in the British isles, moors; in Eastern Europe and Asia, steppes. Local areas also have unique names for grasslands. For example, the grassland area in southeastern Washington state and spilling over into Idaho is called the Palouse.

People use grasslands for farming and ranching, since grasslands have rich soil and can support a large amount of agriculture, particularly if the soil is watered and amended. Grasslands are especially important to the beef and dairy industries.

Wildlife and plant life are abundant in grasslands as well, particularly supporting large herds of herbivorous animals.

Additional Layer

Climate determines what kinds of lands we have to a large degree. Grasslands are usually found in places that are too wet to be deserts, but too dry to be forests. Most of their rainfall comes in a very short time. Grasses are good at surviving in this kind of climate because their stems and leaves have a special way of storing water.

Additional Layer

The rich top soil in some grasslands can be twenty feet or more deep. In contrast, a typical topsoil is less than a foot deep. Deep top soil means that certain invertebrate creatures like mites and worms can thrive in these areas. The Giant Palouse Earthworm lives in soils to a depth of 16 feet and can grow to be at least 3 feet long.

Agriculture has threatened the worm and it was thought for a time to be extinct.

ANCIENT INDIA – GRASSLANDS – ELEMENTS – TEXTURE & FORM

☺ ☺ ☺ **EXPLORATION: Map of Worldwide Grasslands**
Make a map showing where grasslands are located in the world. Use the Grasslands of the World map printable from the end of this unit. You can write in the names people use for grasslands in different parts of the world.

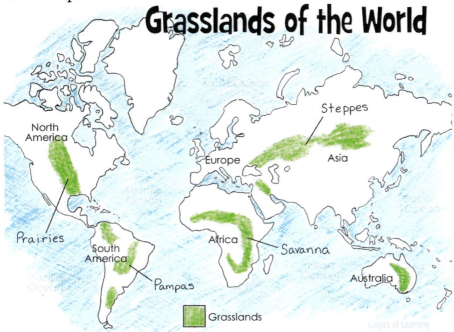

Additional Layer

Fire works well as a management technique for grasslands because grasses grow from the base of the plant instead of from the tip, as in other plants.

This also works out well when supporting grazing animals. If grasses grew from the tip like other plants they would be killed off every time a cow came along, but instead the grasses are unfazed.

☺ ☺ **EXPLORATION: Landform Types in Grasslands**
Here are some types of landforms found in grasslands:
- hills: a gentle rise of ground
- knob: smaller than a hill
- knoll: even smaller than a knob
- meadow: an area of grassland in an otherwise wooded area
- highlands: land that is higher than the surrounding land
- lowlands: the opposite of highlands, these are lands close to sea level.
- plain: a large, mostly level expanse of land covered with grasses for the most part

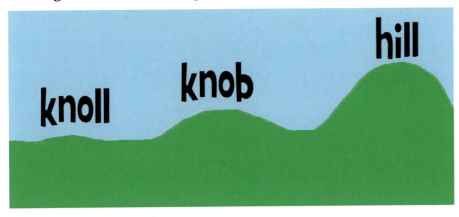

Additional Layer

This is the Prairie Potholes region of the northern Great Plains in Canada and the far northern United States.

The formation of the thousands of tiny lakes and ponds was left behind when the glaciers of the last Ice Age departed.

ANCIENT INDIA – GRASSLANDS – ELEMENTS – TEXTURE & FORM

After learning about some of the landforms found in a grassland, play the Grassland Game. You can print the game board from the end of this unit.

🙂 🟢 EXPLORATION: Rain on the Plain

Grasslands can have extreme weather from icy, windy, cold winters to blazing hot, dusty summers. They can have torrential downpours of rain and they can have droughts that last for months or even decades, threatening all life.

Make a weather box to show what it's like on the plains. First, paint the inside of the box to look like the plains. Green on the bottom with big blue sky above.

Then using a brown or black piece of construction paper cut a circular spiral shape. This you will hang from the top of the box so that it hangs down to the "grass" at the bottom. This is a twister on the plains.

Now cut two slits in the back of your box so that you can send the weather along the back. You'll paint a long sheet of paper in panels so that you have a spring scene with flowers and rain and a cloud covered sky. You can have a summer scene with a blazing hot sun, and no clouds at all. You can have a fall scene with dry dead grass and maybe a grass fire. Then you can have a winter scene with howling wind and long drifts of snow (try using a toothbrush to flick paint on your scene to show snow).

*Alternately you can show the rainy and dry seasons on a tropical grassland.

Fabulous Fact
There are two broad categories of grasslands: temperate and tropical. Temperate grasslands are located in cool places with cold winters and hot summers. Tropical grasslands are hot year round, but usually have a rainy season and a dry season.

Additional Layer
Probably the most difficult aspect of grassland conservation is that the large mammals of the grassland require extensive unfenced range for migration, but there aren't many unfenced places left in the world.

How do you think this problem could be solved?

Heads Up
We'll be covering more about the conservation and ecology of grasslands in the Year Four units.

Additional Layer

Little House on the Prairie by Laura Ingalls Wilder and others in this series give a glimpse of what pioneer life was like on the virgin prairies of North America.

Ancient India – Grasslands – Elements – Texture & Form

😊 🟢 **EXPLORATION: Cultures of Grasslands**
Read one of these books:
Bringing the Rain to Kapiti Plain by Verna Aardema
If You're Not From the Prairie by David Bouchard
Little House on the Prairie by Laura Ingalls Wilder
Sarah, Plain and Tall by Patricia McLachlan

Then learn about the culture of the people who live where the book takes place. *Bringing the Rain to Kapiti Plain* takes place in western Africa on the savanna among the Zulu culture. The other three take place in North America on the Great Plains.

Do a book project to go with the book you chose. Here are some ideas:
- Make a diorama
- Create a Zulu bead design (search the Internet)
- Use yarn to make Zulu *amoShoba*, a sort of skirt of cows' tails worn just below the knees and on the upper arms.
- Make a model of a Zulu *kraal*, or village. Use upside down egg carton sections for the domed huts.
- Make a map showing where the native tribes of Indians lived on the North American plains at the time of European contact.
- Make a model teepee. A kid sized model can be made from fabric and long poles or make a tiny model from paper and toothpicks. A teepee is important to the plains culture because it indicates how the people followed the migratory grazing herds of bison and deer.
- The Great Plains were also the scene of the cattle drives of the old west. Dress up like a cowboy and learn why the Great Plains were so perfect for cattle.
- Look at an image of the Great Plains from an airplane view. Paint a patchwork picture of square fields.
- Write a simulated journal as though you were a settler of the North American plains.

Present your book project to an audience, like your family at dinner time.

😊 🟢 🔵 **EXPEDITION: Grasslands**
Take a trip to a grassland or meadow near you. Take along an insect field guide and a wildflower field guide. Get down and look closely at the different types of grasses and other plants. Sometimes we think of grasslands as one huge monoculture of grass, but it's not. Really wild grasslands are made up of a huge diversity of plants. Nature doesn't tend toward monocultures,

Additional Layer

Here are some paintings of grasslands:

The Buffalo Trail by Albert Bierstadt

Camping on the Prairie by Paul Kane, 1846

Dans la Prairie by Claude Monet, 1876

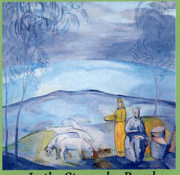
In the Steppe by Pavel Kuznetsov, 1911

Find more by searching for "grasslands paintings" online.

Ancient India – Grasslands – Elements – Texture & Form

Additional Layer

The first North American farmers dug up all the native grasses and planted crops that didn't have strong roots like the grasses. When there wasn't enough rain the soil dried out and the wind blew the topsoil away. There were giant dust clouds. Even worse, without the rich topsoil, crops just wouldn't grow.

Writer's Workshop

Today we keep and create new grasslands for agriculture by burning the grass and grazing animals on the land. Indian tribes used burning for the same purpose to create and maintain more habitat for grazing animals. Ancient and medieval peoples have done the same thing in Europe, Asia and the Americas for thousands of years.

Some people think that any human interference in grasslands is a travesty. Others think without people to make it useful it's just wasted space. How do you think we should treat and use grasslands? Why? Write about your opinion.

since huge swaths of the same plants deplete the soil and invite disease.

Here are some grassland preserves of North America:
- Pawnee National Grassland near Greely, Colorado
- Grasslands National Park in southern Saskatchewan
- Theodore Roosevelt National Park in North Dakota
- Badlands National Park in South Dakota

☺ ☻ EXPLORATION: The African Savannah

Gather some plastic farm animals and African animals (usually found at dollar stores) and head to a grassy area to tell about the Masai and the African Savannah lands. As you tell about the Masai and the wildlife of the Serengheti, move the animals around in herds and imagine together what it would be like to be there. When you are done telling the kids, see how much they can tell back to you.

The Masai people are herders in eastern Africa. They have raised cattle and goats on the savannas for thousands of years. They never stay in the same place for long. They are always moving, going along with the herds to find new grazing lands and fresh water. Masai boys start herding calves when they are just five years old and by the time they are fifteen they have their own herd.

For years the Masai herders were the only people who lived on the Serengheti Plain, but then farmers, ranchers, and hunters arrived. Before the savannah lands could be damaged by all the people, they created Serengheti National Park to protect the millions of animals who live there. If you went there today you could see lions, zebras, cheetahs, wildebeests, and leopards.

☺ ☻ EXPLORATION: The Pampas

Besides being good farmland and natural habitats for animals, grasslands are also perfect grazing land for ranchers and herders. Ranchers in the Pampas of Argentina build big stretches of fences to keep their animals from wandering off. The cowboys who work on the ranches are called gauchos. They ride across the Pampas, mend fences, and round up cattle. When it's time to take them to the market to be sold the gauchos drive the herds into corrals.

Make a Venn diagram and compare U.S. cowboys to Argentine gauchos. How are they the same? How are they different?

Ancient India – Grasslands – Elements – Texture & Form

😊 🟢 EXPLORATION: Leaves of Grass

Make grass blades from paper and write grasslands facts on each blade. You can search the internet for facts about grasses. Here are a few facts to get you started:

- Plains grasses have long roots. They can grow twice as deep underground as they do above ground.
- The roots of grasses tangle up together as they grow. This makes a woven mat that holds the topsoil in place.
- Over the years, overgrazing has hurt the grasslands.
- Much of the land that was once full of grasses and wildflowers is now covered by asphalt and concrete where cities have been built, especially in the grasslands of the United States.
- Common grasslands plants include buffalo grass, cone flowers, sunflowers, crazy weed, asters, and goldenrod.

😊 🟢 EXPLORATION: Crops Grown on Grasslands

Most of the world's food is grown in former grasslands. Make a field mosaic from crop seeds.

You can use dried wheat, corn, peas, soybeans, lentils, beans, barley and sunflower seeds to make a farm scene on construction paper. Just use a paint brush to paint white glue over the paper and glue the seeds on in rows to make farm fields.

😊 🟢 EXPLORATION: A Nature Notebook

Make a nature notebook featuring grassland animals. Use the worksheets at the end of this unit. Then, if you'd like, you can add more grassland animals to your notebook. Each of the pages has a description which your child can trace for cursive handwriting practice if you desire. The descriptions also give them practice with how to write a very short beginning report. You can also add more details of your own as well. You may also color in the pictures.

Additional Layer

For a cool art project to go along with this unit you can grow a grasshead.

Put grass seed in the toe of a knee high nylon stocking. Put a shovel full of potting soil in on top of the grass seed, and tie a knot to hold the seed and soil in a little ball. Now soak the ball in a bowl of water overnight. The next day, fill a jar with water and put the ball on top of the jar, with the end of the nylon hanging down into the water. This will draw water up and keep your grass head moist. Now glue whatever kind of face on you would like, use hot glue or another non-water soluble glue). In about 10 days you will have green grass hair. Anytime the water in the jar gets low, pull the head out to pour a little more water. You can trim it as much or as little as you like, depending upon your preferred hairstyle.

ANCIENT INDIA – GRASSLANDS – ELEMENTS – TEXTURE & FORM

SCIENCE: ELEMENTS

An element is the smallest unit of matter that behaves in a unique manner. Elements are made up of only one kind of atom each. Atoms are made of electrons, protons, and neutrons. Every electron is exactly like every other electron and the same is true of protons and neutrons, but electrons, neutrons, and protons can be combined in a multitude of ways to make different substances that behave in unique ways. For example, hydrogen is made of one electron and one proton. Hydrogen is a colorless, odorless gas that is highly explosive. Lead is made of 82 electrons, 82 protons, and 125 neutrons. Lead is a stable, solid metal at room temperature. The different combinations of electrons, protons, and neutrons make for different "stuff."

The periodic table is a human invention that helps us organize the elements. Because the periodic table is orderly and because the laws of the universe are orderly, the periodic table can help us see the properties of an element and predict how that element will behave in nature and when combined with other elements.

Famous Folks

Dmitri Mendeleev was the first to figure out the periodicity of elements. In other words, he realized there was an order to the elements and was able to put it all together.

Irritatingly, textbooks and other chemistry books for kids call him a "Russian School Teacher." He did teach high school for a short time, but he was first and foremost a brilliant and highly trained experimental chemist who hobnobbed at the universities and was prized by the Tzar.

He *did* have bad hair though, why don't they ever talk about that?

Watch this: http://youtu.be/fPnwBITSmgU

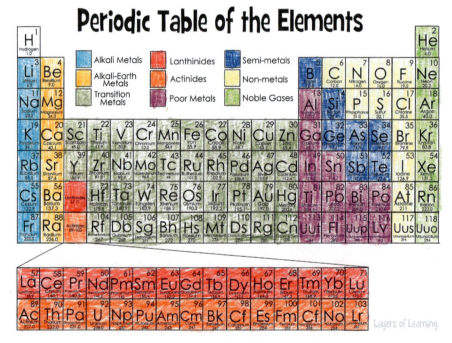

😊 😀 **EXPLORATION: Elemental Cooking Class**

To show the difference between an element and more complex substances like molecules and compounds show the kids the ingredients to make brownies or cookies. Each of the individual ingredients is like the elements. Elements are the ingredients

ANCIENT INDIA – GRASSLANDS – ELEMENTS – TEXTURE & FORM

that make up all the stuff on Earth. Then combine the ingredients, or "elements" to make the tasty treat. This is like hydrogen and oxygen, two gases combining to make water. Elements combine to make molecules.

To take this further, explain that not all the ingredients were combined in equal amounts. You use far more flour than you do baking powder or salt. In the same way, the elements are not equal in nature. Hydrogen and helium are the most common elements in the universe as a whole. Oxygen and silicon are the most common elements in the earth's crust. Carbon, hydrogen, and oxygen are the most common elements found in the human body.

☺ ☺ ☺ **EXPLORATION: Colors of the Periodic Table**
Print out a black and white copy of the periodic table and a table showing the elements colored according to "families." The families are groups of elements that behave in similar ways. Have the kids color their tables to match the families on the colored copy. Both a black and white and colored copy of the periodic table can be found at the end of this unit.

After coloring and labeling the families, learn these rules of the periodic table:

- Periods run horizontally across the table and the atomic number goes up one as you move from right to left. The atomic number is the number of protons in an atom. The atomic number is the large number at the top of the box for a particular element.
- Groups run vertically down the table and all elements in a particular group have the same number of electrons in their outer shell, so they behave in similar ways.
- The letters in each box are a symbol for the chemical. The symbol for carbon is C, the symbol for lead is Pb and comes from the Latin for lead which is plumbum. The elements are given "Latinized" names to make them sound like Latin, even though most of them are not.
- The number at the bottom of the elements box is the atomic weight, or total weight of protons, neutrons, and electrons for that element. Hydrogen, which has one proton and one electron has a weight of 1. (The weight of electrons compared to protons and neutrons is negligible and not really counted.)

With your middle grades and high school kids, watch this video from Mr. Anderson: http://youtu.be/fLSfgNxoVGk. And this one

On The Web
http://www.ptable.com/
Click this link for an interactive periodic table.

Fabulous Fact
Only ninety of the elements on the periodic table occur in nature. The rest of them, mostly the heaviest elements only exist in a lab. Some of the man-made elements are useful in medicine and technology, but others are so fleeting that they have no uses whatsoever.

For Your Teen
Learn about the Periodic Table with Khan Academy:
https://www.khanacademy.org/science/chemistry/periodic-table-trends-bonding

Also, read chapter 3 of *A Self-Teaching Guide: Chemistry* by Houk.

Fabulous Fact
Believe it or not the stodgy technical periodic table has been the scene of much controversy and strife. Arguments over who discovered what first, and therefore who gets to do the naming, are the most common. Such disputes are decided by the International Union of Pure Applied Chemistry (IUPAC).

Ancient India – Grasslands – Elements – Texture & Form

Famous Folks

Learn about John Dalton who first discovered that elements are made up of a single type of atom.

Additional Layer

Scientists can make brand new elements by bombarding an atom with protons in a linear accelerator, though none of these artificial elements are stable. Some are used in medicine and technological applications though. Adding a proton makes a new element. Learn more about particle accelerators.

from Crash Course: http://youtu.be/oRRVV4Diomg

After you've explained the basic rules of the periodic table, quiz the kids, giving rewards for good performance.

Some examples of quiz questions:

- Which family does Xenon (Xe) belong to?
- What is the chemical symbol for gold?
- How many electrons are in the outer shell of Boron (B)?
- Name an element in the same group with Carbon.
- Which element has the chemical symbol Na?
- How many electrons are in the outer shell of the Halogen gases?

You get the idea. This exercise is not intended to help kids memorize the periodic table, but rather to learn what the symbols mean and how to interpret them, so they can reference the table when they need information later.

Just in case you do want to memorize, or at least become more familiar with, the periodic table try this, played repeatedly ad nauseum, should do it: http://youtu.be/-I7l8TgtuLQ

☺ ☺ ☺ **EXPLORATION: More Coloring Fun**

At normal temperatures on Earth most elements are solid, which makes sense if you think about it, seeing as the Earth itself is pretty solid and all. Color the periodic table to show which states of matter each element is in at normal Earth temperatures.

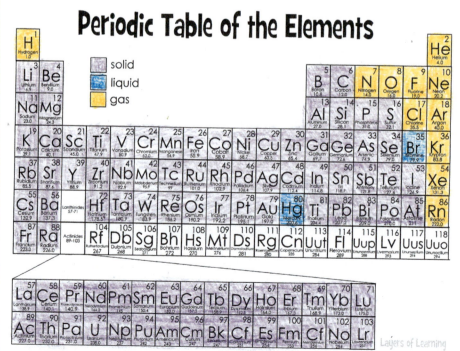

ANCIENT INDIA – GRASSLANDS – ELEMENTS – TEXTURE & FORM

A few of the elements are left uncolored. These are laboratory produced elements that were made in such miniscule amounts and were so fleeting that we don't even know their normal state.

Want to see which elements are essential to the human body and which are poisons? Take a look at the table below. We labeled the essential nutrients in pink, the poisons in green, and the radioactive poisons in yellow.

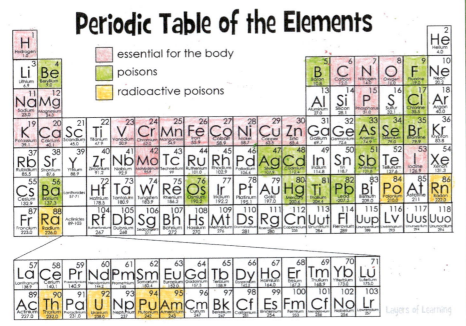

Actually everything after number 92 (Uranium) is radioactive, but most of these elements exist in such tiny quantities on Earth that you'll never be exposed to them. In addition, we left unlabeled several elements that are toxic in isotopic forms, but not toxic in their normal state, like Cobalt-60 and Strontium-90. Also, fascinatingly, some of the essential nutrients are toxic in any but trace amounts, like Vanadium, Chromium, and Copper. Fluorine is a decided toxin and yet in certain forms and trace amounts it appears to aid greatly in healthy teeth. Most of the elements left blank neither help nor harm as they are simply not able to be absorbed by the body at all.

We can divide the periodic table into stable and radioactive elements as well. Everything up to Lead (Pb) is stable, with the exception of Technetium (Tc) and Promethium (Pm). Everything after that is radioactive. Radioactivity means the atom is shedding parts like a shaggy dog in spring. Atoms can grow too big, too unwieldy, too high energy. The solution is to get rid of some neutrons and protons from the nucleus. (More about radioactivity in Unit 1-15).

Fabulous Fact
An element's chemistry, or the way it behaves in reactions, is determined mostly by how many valence electrons it has. Valence electrons are the electrons in the outer shell of an atom, the electrons that are available for use. You can tell how many valence electrons an atom has by looking at the periodic table. The elements in column one have one valence electron, the elements in column two have two valence electrons. Then we skip over to column 13 where the elements have three valence electrons and so on to the end of the table.

Fabulous Fact
It's no accident that Superman can't see through lead. Lead is the last stable (non-radioactive) element on the periodic table. It also is used regularly as shielding from radiation.

Fabulous Fact
The periodic table isn't static. Scientists keep refining it and discovering new elements.

ANCIENT INDIA – GRASSLANDS – ELEMENTS – TEXTURE & FORM

Fabulous Fact

Technetium, meaning artificial, was one of the most difficult elements to discover. Its existence was predicted by Dmitri Mendeleev long before its actually discovery, though chemists were striving hard to become the discoverer, thus gaining immortality and perhaps a Nobel prize. There were three false discoveries of technetium before the actual discovery. The problem is its unexpected radioactivity. No other element so high on the periodic table is radioactive. In fact, the only source of technetium used in medicines today is artificial sources, thus the name.

No one really knows why Technetium or Promethium are radioactive in a sea of stable elements. Physicists (once you leave chemical reactions and begin to talk about how atoms behave you exit chemistry and enter physics) have ideas with long technical names like the "semi-empirical mass formula" based upon the "liquid drop model" and involving lots of calculations of parabolas and other calculus type math, but actually up to now they're just guessing.

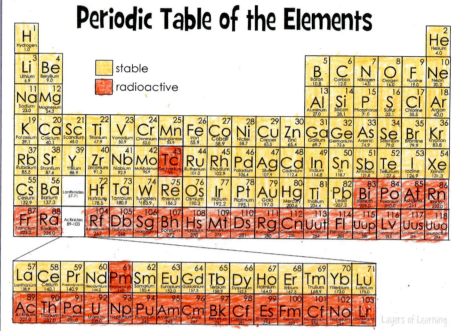

Everything after Uranium on the periodic table is so radioactive that barely any, if any at all, exist in nature.

☺ ☺ ☺ EXPLORATION: Playing Games Periodically

Play one of these games to improve familiarity with the periodic table:

- Element Hang Man: pick an element name and play hangman with it. Let the kids use the periodic table as reference. They'll be searching all over trying to find the correct element and becoming more familiar with the periodic table in the process.
- Element Bingo: have each student fill in a five by five bingo chart with the names of elements from the periodic table. Place the element symbols into a sack and pick out and read the symbols. The kids will have to match the names to the symbols. Again, let them use the periodic table as a reference. You can also use the atomic numbers instead and have them match numbers to symbols or names.
- Element Concentration: Have two sets of cards, one with the name of the element and one with the chemical symbol. Turn them all upside down and play a matching game, taking turns turning over two cards at a time. Use the periodic table as a reference.
- Element Crossword Puzzles: Use graph paper and have the kids make a cross word puzzle with the element symbols as clues and the element names as answers. Have them swap and complete each others' puzzles.

Ancient India – Grasslands – Elements – Texture & Form

☺ ☺ ☺ **EXPLORATION: Alkali Metals and a Potassium Feast**

The alkali metals are really reactive metals. They don't occur freely in nature. These metals have only one electron in their outer shell. Therefore, they are ready to lose that one electron in ionic bonding with other elements. Like other metals, alkali metals are malleable, ductile, and are good conductors of heat and electricity. They're softer than most other metals though. Lithium, sodium, potassium, rubidium, cesium, and francium make up the alkali metals and are found in group 1 on the periodic table. Cesium and francium are the most reactive elements in this group.

Watch the alkali metals react: http://youtu.be/GVoJZkmAAfA

In 1807 Humphrey Davy, a chemist and poet, was separating melted potash from wood ashes. This led to his discovery of three important elements all within a few weeks' time: potassium, sodium, and calcium. He named potassium after the potash he found it in. Then, to honor the German and Scandinavian word for potash, Kalium, it was given the symbol "K."

Potassium is an important part of our diet. Because our bodies can't store it, we need a constant intake of it to avoid fatigue, arthritis, and thyroid problems. Potassium also helps maintain the fluid balance within our bodies. Have a potassium feast by eating some of these foods that are rich in potassium: cashews, almonds, bananas, spinach, potatoes, apricots, kiwi, avocados, milk, oranges, orange juice, honeydew melon, and yogurt.

☺ ☺ **EXPLORATION: Alkaline-Earth Metals, Beryllium, and Emeralds, Oh My!**

Alkaline-Earth metals are very reactive, so they are never found all on their own in nature. Beryllium, magnesium, calcium, strontium, barium, and radium make up this group.

Watch some reactions in this group: http://youtu.be/dUbjn3ix3ds
The chemistry teacher doing this video compares the alkaline-earths to the alkali metals.

Beryllium is a rare element, both on the earth and in our universe in general. It isn't necessary for plant or animal life. Beryllium was discovered by Nicolas-Louis Vauquelin in 1798 within an emerald. You can buy inexpensive raw emeralds on eBay to clean. Just use a dremmel tool, toothbrushes, small picks, or similar instruments to remove the debris and make the emeralds glisten.

Definitions

<u>Malleable</u>: can be pounded flat or into other shapes when heated.

<u>Ductile</u>: can be drawn out into a thin wire.

<u>Conductor</u>: electrons can flow through it, taking electricity from one place to another.

Famous Folks

Humphrey Davy discovered potassium, sodium, calcium, magnesium, boron, and barium. Besides being a chemist, Humphrey Davy was also a public speaker, poet, traveler, scholar, and an inventor. There had been several explosions from ignited methane and other gases in the coal mines that had been causing casualties. He saw how dangerous work for miners had become and thought of a solution. He invented the Davy Lamp, which separated the flame from the gases with wire gauze.

Fig. 192. Davysche Sicherheitslampe

Ancient India – Grasslands – Elements – Texture & Form

Explanation

Kids need manipulatives to help them conceptualize and understand the abstract concepts happening in their math homework. Most kids, because of the developmental stage of their minds, cannot grasp abstract concepts until they are in around 5th or 6th grade. Young kids need to see the crayons they are adding or the halves of an apple, then around third or fourth grade they are able to imagine the apple halves. It's not until late elementary or the beginning of junior high that they can add numbers without reference to concrete objects at all.

Michelle

Additional Layer

Go on a trash hunt. Give teams bags to try to fill as fast as they can at a location in your town that needs to be spruced up.

Have a re-use invention convention. Find some items around your house that normally get thrown away (like food packaging) and re-use them to create some cool inventions. You could even make it a contest.

☺ ☺ ☺ EXPLORATION: Transition Metals and Titanium

There are thirty-eight transition metals, including copper, iron, nickel, silver, mercury, gold, and titanium. These metals are malleable and ductile, and they also conduct heat and electricity.

Titanium was discovered by William Gregor in England in 1791. He was a pastor and an amateur geologist who recognized he had found something uncatalogued, but wasn't entirely sure how to isolate the element. He turned over the information to a geological society and a science journal. Not long afterward, Martin Klaproth independently discovered the element as well, and he named it titanium after the titans, predecessors to the Greek gods.

Titanium, photo by USGS

Titanium is a shiny, dark metal that is lightweight, very strong, and resistant to acid. It's the 9th most abundant element in the crust of the earth, but isn't naturally found on its own. It is bonded to other metals, and interestingly, people typically use it as an alloy combined with other metals as well.

Because of its properties, it is useful for a lot of products, often as an alloy. Make a collage of items that contain titanium. Here are a few:

jewelry
medical prosthesis
dental implants
cars
certain kinds of paint
airplanes
missiles
ships

bicycles
computers
jewelry
golf clubs
tennis racquets
motorcycles
knives
submarines

☺ ☺ ☺ EXPLORATION: Other Metals

This group includes aluminum, gallium, indium, tin, thallium, lead, and bismuth – all solid, opaque metals with a high density.

Ancient India – Grasslands – Elements – Texture & Form

Aluminum is plentiful. It is the most abundant metal in the earth's crust, and the third most abundant element on the planet (oxygen and silicon take first and second). It was discovered by Hans Christian Oersted in 1825, and was once considered to be a precious metal. Napoleon III was said to have held a banquet during which his most important guests ate from aluminum utensils while all the less-thans had to make do with simple gold ones. Now we often throw it out like garbage! Aluminum is a soft, lightweight metal that is malleable and non-magnetic.

Here are a few tidbits about the most recycled package in America: aluminum cans.
- It's estimated that since the early 1970's over 25 million TONS of aluminum cans have been recycled. If you placed that many cans end to end it could stretch to the moon more than 482 times!
- We currently recycle about 53% of the aluminum cans we use in the United States In 1972 (when we started recycling aluminum) we recycled 53 million pounds of aluminum cans. That's less than we recycle in a week currently (we only recycle about 47% of the cans we use).
- When a can is recycled it's back on the shelf as a new can in less than 2 months.
- The weight of aluminum cans recycled in 2009 was 807,860 tons . . . about as much as 11 or 12 aircraft carriers (more aircraft carriers than the U.S. owns).
- We save 95% of the production energy when we recycle a can rather than making a brand new one from ore. That means that 16.1 million barrels of oil were saved due to aluminum can recycling in 2009.
- Some places still buy back recycled pop cans. Since 1972 Americans have earned quite a bit from selling back aluminum cans – over $33 billion.

Start your own recycling project. Gather aluminum cans, cardboard, newspapers, junk mail, and glass, and recycle it in your community. Aluminum is especially neat for recycling because it is 100% recyclable without losing any of its qualities. Even one kid can make a difference.

☺ ☺ ☺ **EXPLORATION: Metalloids and Silly Silicon**
Silicon is a metalloid, or an element that has properties of both metals and non-metals. It is found in all kinds of things around us, from sand to computer wires, and from calculators to glass. It's in the sun, the stars, and many meteorites that have made it to the earth. Because it's a good conductor of electricity, it is used in computer chips and other technological components. That's

Writer's Workshop
Write a persuasive essay or letter to the editor about the importance of recycling and cleaning up our planet. You may even organize a clean-up project to do that can be included in your essay or letter.

On the Web
They Might Be Giants and the periodic table of the elements . . . can't go wrong there: http://youtu.be/dozION8xjbM

Additional Layer
The reason aluminum went from rare to abundant was an American named Charles Martin Hall, who discovered how to easily extract the aluminum from ore containing it, just in time for WWI and the advent of the airplane.

This new-found abundance and the havoc it created with the value of Napoleon's dinner plates is a great example of how supply affects prices in an open market.

By the way, only Americans spell aluminum with one "i." Everyone else in the world spells it aluminium. We can thank Hall for that as well.

Ancient India – Grasslands – Elements – Texture & Form

Additional Layer

A favorite dream of science fiction writers is the silicon based life on other planets. This is because silicon is just one box down from carbon on the periodic table and has many of the same chemical properties: four bond locations, bonds well with metals and non-metals, is a solid at normal temperatures, etc.

The problem is that carbon can make beautiful organic bendy helical bonds in long chains (proteins and sugars). Carbon can also bond with oxygen to make a gas, easily incorporated into living things like plants. Silicon can't do either of these very important things because it carries too much baggage. All those extra electrons in extra shells makes silicon unwieldy and stiff in bonding, and prevents it from ever forming a gas in compound.

To be a silicon based life form, one would have to literally breathe sand constantly, the way we breathe air. (But that too would make an excellent sci-fi creature, don't you think?)

how the Santa Clara Valley near San Francisco, California got its nickname – Silicon Valley. The chips and components were largely manufactured in that area, and it became known as the center of computer technology.

Perhaps my favorite application of silicon is the famous Silly Putty. It was invented by two men in the same year. James Wright created some quite accidentally when he dropped boric acid into silicone oil by mistake. Earl Warrick also made it, this time on purpose, as he was trying to create a synthetic rubber. It is incredibly bouncy and stretchy, and even copies newspaper print on to itself. Because it is bonded together with hydrogen, it has some interesting properties. When a bit of pressure is applied to it, only some of the hydrogen bonds are broken and the putty stretches and flows. However, if a lot of pressure is put on them, all the hydrogen bonds break and the putty tears like a solid. When Peter Hodgson, an unemployed copyright, saw the silicon putty, he bought its rights, named it Silly Putty, and put it in plastic eggs to sell for the upcoming Easter holiday. It has been a popular toy ever since.

You can pick up some Silly Putty from the store and try out some of its unique characteristics, or you can make your own. You can't use the actual chemicals to create silly putty at home because they are too dangerous, but here's a safer version that's easy to make:

Combine 2 parts Elmer's white glue with 1 part liquid starch. If it's a bit too sticky, add more starch as needed. You can also change its color by adding a few drops of food coloring. Cover and refrigerate it when you aren't using it.

☺ ☺ ☺ **EXPERIMENT: Carbon Detective, The Search For Non-Metals**

Non-metals can't conduct heat or electricity very well at all. They are brittle and therefore, can't be pounded into sheets or rolled into wires like metallic elements. At room temperature they are usually gases or solids. Oxygen, hydrogen, and carbon are some of the most plentiful elements on the planet, and they are all non-metals.

Carbon is abundant throughout the universe and was discovered in ancient times. It is an essential part of what makes life possible on Earth. Because carbon can bond with itself in strong and stable chains, it is an excellent building block for living things. It also bonds well with other non-metals. Carbon, hydrogen, and oxygen form complex chains of carbohydrates, the

Ancient India – Grasslands – Elements – Texture & Form

building blocks of life. As far as we know, all living things contain carbon. Now it's time to be a carbon detective and look at the carbon within some living things. You'll need:

- a candle and some matches
- a piece of paper
- a pencil
- leaves
- sugar
- a metal can lid
- some tongs

First, light the candle. Now hold the metal lid over the flame using the set of tongs. After a bit you'll see a black substance on the lid (soot). Soot is actually carbon. Now use the pencil to scribble heavy and dark on the piece of paper, Rub your finger over the scribble and take a look at your finger – you guessed it! That's carbon. Next, burn some paper and leaves in a safe area, like a fire pit. What happens to them? Can you spot the carbon? Finally, put some sugar on a can lid and heat it up. What happens to the sugar?

The paper, leaves, and sugar all turned black. You were burning materials which were once living. When the burning is over, all that's left is the carbon, the black substance you saw.

☺ ☺ ☺ **EXPLORATION: Halogens**

Halogen means salt-former. All the halogens, including fluorine, chlorine, iodine, bromine, and astatine contain salt. The salt in seawater is not actually just sodium (or Na); it is NaCl (See the Cl part? That's chlorine.) That's where you find chlorine most commonly, but in its gas form it is incredibly toxic. In fact, chlorine was used as a weapon during World War I. Bottles were filled with the green gas and then thrown at the enemy. When the bottles landed they exploded, and the toxic gas was released.

Today it's used mostly to keep things clean. It's one of the ingredients of bleach, and also used to keep swimming pools sanitary. There are a lot of experiments that can be done with chlorine, but because of its toxicity, we recommend watching the demonstrations rather than actually conducting your own experiment. If you go to You Tube you can see all kinds of experiments from the reaction of Sodium and Chlorine to the explosions of chlorine gas bombs. Search for "chlorine experiments." Start here: http://youtu.be/FDIx_TyPeeU

Additional Layers

Topsoil is darker than the soil below it because it is full of rotten plants and animals. The carbon from these living things gives the soil its dark color.

Carbon is such an important part of life on our planet that it has its very own branch of science called Organic Chemistry.

Conspiracy Theory on the Periodic Table

Fluorine is the cause of much controversy. Is adding fluorine to our drinking water one of the cheapest and greatest public health measures ever taken or is it an evil plot by industry and government to kill the public through slow poisoning? See, fluorine is definitely and undeniably one of the most toxic elements on Earth. The reason it was added to the drinking water was that observations were made and then tests run showing that people who lived where fluorine naturally occurred in their drinking water had healthier teeth.

Learn more for yourself. http://en.wikipedia.org/wiki/Water_fluoridation_controversy

Ancient India – Grasslands – Elements – Texture & Form

Fabulous Fact

The noble gases were discovered late in the fill-the-periodic-table game chemists played through the 1800's and 1900's. This is because they don't react. They're not found in any compounds and they are all gases. They are colorless and odorless and do absolutely nothing without severe provocation.

On the Web

Look for You Tube videos about the noble gases. Here are some we like:

http://youtu.be/QLrofyj6a2s

http://youtu.be/N71VoBdP_r8

Additional Layer

When sounds are sped up through a stereo they also create a higher pitch because of the faster sound waves. That's the magic of *Alvin and the Chipmunks*.

Expedition

Most elements on the periodic table are metals. Take a tour of a mine. If that's not possible, visit the Stillwater Palladium Mine online:

www.stillwatermining.com

☺ ☺ ☺ **EXPLORATION: Noble and Squeaky Gases**

Noble gases are the most stable of the elements. Their outer electron shells are full, so they aren't looking to share electrons with other elements. They include neon, argon, krypton, radon, xenon, and helium.

Helium was actually discovered on the sun before it was ever isolated on Earth. Two men, Pierre-Jules-César Janssen, a French astronomer, and Sir Norman Lockyer, a British astronomer, noticed a yellow line in the chromosphere of the sun while studying a total solar eclipse in 1868 and realized that this line at its specific wavelength could not be produced by any element known at the time. Lockyer named the element helium for the god of the sun, Helios.

We use helium for inflating blimps and balloons (both scientific balloons and party balloons). Scuba divers use it in combination with oxygen for their breathing tanks. And of course, we all use it to make our voices sound funny.

Get a party balloon full of helium and breathe in the gas. Despite rumors to the contrary, this isn't harmful and doesn't hurt your vocal chords. When you speak with the helium your voice will sound high-pitched and squeaky. The cool thing is that your voice isn't really changing at all. Only the sound has changed. You see, helium isn't as dense at the air you normally breathe, so it allows the sound waves to travel more quickly through it. The lighter the air, the faster the sound waves, and the faster the sound waves, the higher the pitch.

*WARNING: Breathing helium from a party balloon isn't harmful because it is combined with oxygen and isn't under pressure, but breathing it directly from a helium tank is not safe!

☺ ☺ ☺ **EXPLORATION: Lanthanides**

Often called rare-earth elements, these elements can be found from numbers 57 to 71 on the periodic table, plus number 39, Yttrium. You've probably confusedly noticed that the lanthanides and the actinides, just below, are in two separate rows below the periodic table. They are situated there so that our table fits on a nice reasonable rectangle of space instead of a long runway stretching impossibly far across our limited paper. These two rows could be inserted into their proper place, but it's inconvenient.

The lanthanides are grouped together because they have similar

ANCIENT INDIA – GRASSLANDS – ELEMENTS – TEXTURE & FORM

chemistry due to the arrangement of their electrons. They are used for dating rocks on Earth and from space, as catalysts when producing glass, production of alloys and magnets, lasers, television optics, night vision goggles and radar, plus more. In addition, these elements are also found together in somewhat rare deposits of Earth, though that's not exactly why they're called rare earth elements (the chemical term "earth" meant something entirely different in the 1800's than it does today). Besides, they're not nearly so rare as was first thought at their discovery.

The first of these elements found was Yttrium, named after the village in Sweden where the first deposits containing it were found. Ytterby, pronounced "iterbee," is a tiny village on a tiny island with a quarry. The following lanthanides were all discovered from samples taken from this quarry: yttrium (Y), ytterbium (Yb), terbium (Tb), erbium (Er) (all named after Ytterby), holmium (named after Stockholm), thulium (named after Thule, a mythic name for Scandinavia), and gadolinium (after the chemist Johan Gadolin).

Color the Lanthanides in on a blank periodic table. Now on a world map, see the printables at the end of this unit, mark the locations of rare earth mines and some of the locations of rare earth deposits that are not currently mined.

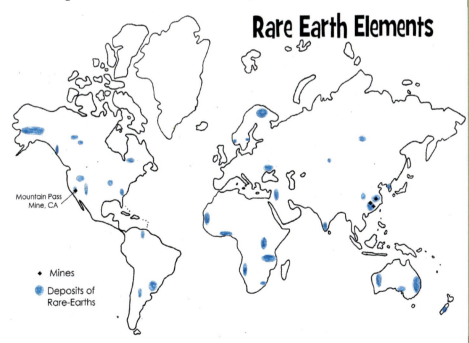

You can see more by going to the USGS site here:
http://mrdata.usgs.gov/mineral-resources/ree.html

Additional Layer

Rare earth elements are essential to modern life. We use them in our iPhones, televisions, toxic energy-efficient light bulbs, computers, and electric motors. The so-called "green" industries rely on them heavily, and somewhat ironically since the mining of these metals is a truly dirty business.

Most of the rare earth elements are controlled by China, either mines in China or mines in Africa, owned by Chinese companies and government agencies. There are deposits of rare earth elements elsewhere, such as in Idaho, but mining for them is forbidden by the U.S. government due to the environmental impact of such mining.

So we blissfully let the oh-so-environmentally conscious* (not to mention militarily friendly) Chinese mine our rare-earths and we implement them in our "clean" ultra modern technologies like Toyota Prius's and wind turbines, without bothering to come up with cleaner mining methods, or recycling programs.

*note above sarcasm

ANCIENT INDIA – GRASSLANDS – ELEMENTS – TEXTURE & FORM

The Arts: Texture & Form

Additional Layer

Meret Oppenheim was part of the surrealist movement. The surrealists purposely place objects where they shouldn't be or in ways they shouldn't be, like a fur covered spoon. Their goal was to force people to think more carefully about reality as opposed to just moving along with their culture.

A lot of people thought the surrealists were just plain crazy, but you have to admit a fur covered spoon makes you think about spoons in a whole new way.

Search for Oppenheim's fur covered spoon online to see images.

Famous Folks

Margaret Roseman is a modern Canadian artist who uses texture in her watercolor paintings. You can view her art at www.margaretroseman.com

Look for her painting *Winter Stream* and compare the texture of the water with the snow and the trees.

Texture, another element of art, is unique because it utilizes not just the sense of sight, but also the sense of touch. However, we don't need to touch a metal mixing bowl to know that its texture is hard and smooth. We don't need to touch a crumpled up piece of paper to know what its texture is like. The variety of angles and planes allow us to feel its texture in our minds without even touching it. Texture evokes emotion in us much in the same way color does. Imagine the feel of a soft fleece blanket and a chain linked fence – can you feel the difference in the emotion that the two textures bring up?

In art, texture can be actual or implied. In some pieces, especially sculpture, the viewer may actually touch the surface, whether smooth, rough, spiky, slick, or slimy. Do a Google image search for Meret Oppenheim's famous fur covered cup, saucer, and spoon. Can you imagine that feeling on your tongue? Paintings, not intended to be touched, can also have texture. Some artists use thick paint to create actual texture, while others master making the objects look textured and realistic through their techniques. Texture gives us an idea of how an object would feel if we could touch it.

Volume, or form, refers to actual 3-D shapes, and in art, this is usually a sculpture.

☺ ☺ ☺ **EXPEDITION: Texture Hunt**

Walk around your home, neighborhood, or a store and try to find objects that have each of these textures:

hairy	soft	rough
slimy	sticky	sharp
silky	smooth	spongy
greasy	fluffy	dry
wet	hard	scratchy

☺ ☺ ☺ **EXPLORATION: Go Go Gadget Painting**

Texture in paintings creates visual interest. A solid blue panel isn't very captivating at all, but add unique textures to the very same blue and it will be fascinating. Try creating unique textured paintings with various gadgets.

First, tape a piece of paper down to the table. Paint a smooth, even layer using one color of finger paint. Cover the entire paper. Next, press some objects into the wet paint and then lift them off.

Ancient India – Grasslands – Elements – Texture & Form

Use q-tips, sponges, a potato masher, wadded up pieces of paper, leaves, or anything else you can find that will leave a textured impression. You can repeat the designs to create patterns and make it even more interesting.

☺ ☺ EXPEDITION: Illustrated Textures
Go to the library to look at childrens' books. Often interesting textures can be found within their illustrations. Look at books by Garth Williams, the d'Aulaires, Maurice Sendak, or Robert Lawson.

☺ ☺ ☺ EXPLORATION: Sketch-And-Etch
Sometimes implied texture can be created just by the way you put lines together on the page. Lines aren't always straight; they can be wavy, jagged, or circular. When we repeat lines over and over again, we create implied texture.

First, color a dark rectangle of crayon on a sheet of paper. Make the crayon sketching very heavy and solid. You can choose just one color or many colors, but the rectangle must be solid and completely filled in.

In a small dish, combine a few drops of dish soap with a few tablespoons of black tempera paint. The soap will help the paint adhere to the waxy crayon surface. Next, cover the crayon rectangle with a layer of the black tempera paint mixture.

While the paint is drying, sketch a simple, repetitive design in your sketchbook. It can be just repeating lines or you can create a picture that includes repetition of lines. For example, you may draw a flower with spiral shapes on the petals, stripes along the stem, and wavy lines on the leaves.

Once the paint is dry, use a straightened paper clip to etch your design on to the painted rectangle. The paint will scratch away, revealing the crayon colors below.

Your picture is flat and doesn't include much real texture, but the repetition of lines will have created an implied texture. In art, we call the implied texture from repeated lines *rhythm*.

☺ ☺ ☺ EXPLORATION: Batik
Batik is a technique where you block out certain areas, much like a stencil blocks out areas that don't get painted. First, paint a large simple shape (like a kite, a tree, or a crescent moon with stars around it) on a sheet of paper using rubber cement. Let it dry.

Additional Layer
The newest frontier in art texture is in creating digital texture for video games and computer animated movies. People who do this are called texture artists.

Compare the textures in animated movies like Disney's *Dumbo* (1941) and Disney's *Ratatouille* (2007).

Additional Layer
Like color, texture elicits an emotional response. Think about how you feel stepping out of a bath onto a smooth, shiny floor versus stepping out onto a shaggy, thick rug. It's not just the physical feel of coldness or smoothness, there's an emotional response as well. Some people love wood in furniture and floors and walls for its warmth. They don't really mean that it's physically warmer. They're describing an emotional feeling they get with wood. Other people prefer steel on countertops and furniture legs. They say it feels clean and sophisticated.

Look through some home magazines and see what you like. What emotional responses do you have to different materials?

Ancient India – Grasslands – Elements – Texture & Form

Additional Layer

Batik began as a hobby for wealthy women in Indonesia. Their designs depicted their families and geographical regions in particular. Today many people still believe certain batik designs can bring luck, wealth, health, and other good fortunes.

Additional Layer

Batik is often used on fabrics which are then made into sarongs. Use an old sheet to create a sarong. Design your own. You could use a batik or tie dye design, or just use fabric markers to draw repeated patterns.

Additional Layer

Several years ago our family had portraits taken. We had one of the photos blown up and glued onto a canvas covered frame. The texture of the painting came through the photograph paper creating the illusion that the photograph was actually a painting.

What other times do people create pretend textures and why?

Now, use quick brushstrokes to paint a layer of watercolor paint over the entire paper in swirling patterns, and let that dry. Once it's dry, rub and peel off the rubber cement. The swirling creates texture and the blocking out with the rubber cement is the batik technique.

EXPLANATION: A Texture Lesson At My House

Today we did an exploration on texture, and it all started with a brainstorm. We brainstormed every texture word we could think of: rough, smooth, slimy, scaly, sharp, bumpy, sticky, and on and on and on. We wrote each of those on a slip of paper. One by one we drew out the slips of paper and handed each one to a kid. They had 2 assignments: (1) Go find something that had that texture, and (2) draw a picture of that texture. Before we were sent off on our assignments we took a quick look at an example though.

I showed the kids *Young Hare* by Durer.

I asked: How would this rabbit feel if you were to touch it? (Soft, furry) Then I had them touch it. Hmmm, it felt just like the piece of paper it was printed on. Not at all soft and furry in fact! It felt slick and smooth. That launched a great discussion about the difference between texture in real life and texture in paintings.

Ancient India – Grasslands – Elements – Texture & Form

We looked closer at the techniques and tricks Durer used so we would "feel" the softness of the rabbit just by looking at it. His work is a perfect example of this because of the incredible detail he put into each bit of fur.

Then the kids were off. They each took their texture word and found something in the house to represent it. Then they made pictures that included those implied textures. My son really latched on to the assignment and found our scaly goldfish and then drew a fish with crayon, going back over it with oil pastels to make each individual textured scale.

Using the two different layered media really added to the depth and texture of his picture. At the dinner table we almost always have a discussion involving what we learned that day. Tonight my four-year-old daughter started and said, "Rabbits are furry, and even if they aren't really, we can draw them so they are!" Well said, Isabel. Lesson learned. I think.

Karen

😊 😊 😊 EXPLORATION: Impasto

Vincent Van Gogh was not well-known during his lifetime, but today he is one of the most famous painters of all time. He only lived a short time, but painted around 800 pictures. In a letter he wrote to his brother, Theo, he said, "I am functioning like a painting engine." Although he was very ill during the final years of his life, his last paintings are thought to be his best. He is known most for his impasto style filled with hatch strokes and rolling, pulsing motions of his paintbrush. Van Gogh would stroke his paint on the canvas with a knife or brush – almost like working with clay, the paint strokes forming textured

Definitions

<u>Physical texture</u>: the piece actually does have real texture that you can touch and feel with your hand.

<u>Visual texture</u>: the texture is shown using painting techniques but if you were to touch the painting or other work you would just feel smooth paper or canvas.

<u>Implied texture</u>: imaginary texture without a real-life corollary. It is used in abstract art most often.

Famous Folks

In the 17th century the ability to portray textures, particularly in fabric, was considered the defining characteristic of a fine artist. Anthony van Dyck mastered the art admirably.

Portrait of Philadelphia and Elisabeth Cary by Anthony van Dyck

Ancient India – Grasslands – Elements – Texture & Form

Famous Folks

Vincent Van Gogh was a Dutch painter who lived during the second half of the 1800's.

Learn more about Van Gogh and look at many examples of his art. We recommend *Van Gogh Paintings: 24 Cards,* art postcards from Dover Publishers.

Use the cards to practice recognizing Van Gogh's style. Mix them with other artists and see if the kids can pick out which ones are Van Gogh's.

There's Burlap in my Paint

Some artists take texture a step further, actually using stuff like string, burlap, newspaper, foil and other materials in their paintings. See work by Jasper Johns, Alberto Burri, and Antoni Taipes.

marks. One of his most famous works, *Sunflowers*, utilized this technique. He actually painted many sunflower paintings.

Prepare your own impasto: In ½ cup of medium thick tempera paint, add one tablespoon of *white detergent powder. Stir until mixed.

*Other thickeners that can be used in place of the detergent include cornstarch and flour. You may need to adjust the recipe a bit to make it the thickness you like.

You'll need to prepare a separate cup of impasto for each paint color you'd like to use. Scoop dollops of paint on to white poster board using wooden craft sticks. Make textures, lines, and shapes in the paint using a variety of tools – craft sticks, straws, pipe cleaners, a toothbrush, paintbrushes, and other similar tools. Let it dry overnight or for several days.

Impasto paintings have two elements of texture – the actual bumpiness of the paint and also the strong implied texture. You can sense the texture Van Gogh created in Sunflowers without actually touching the original painting at all.

☺ ☺ ☺ **EXPLORATION: Clay and Plaster Bas Relief**

Bas (pronounced "bah") is a French word that means "low." Relief means it is being raised from the background. Take a look at a nickel. Notice how the figures actually stick up from the background of the coin? This is relief. Artists create molds and then create sculptures using the relief molds.

You can do that too. First, press some clay into the bottom of a flat box (like a shoe box). Make the clay about an inch thick. Now press gadgets into the clay to create textures and patterns in the clay. Next, mix up a batch of Plaster of Paris, The plaster should be creamy. Pour the plaster into the clay mold about 2 inches deep. Tap the sides of the box to remove air bubbles. Let it dry and harden for several days.

Ancient bas relief sculpture from Persepolis.

Ancient India – Grasslands – Elements – Texture & Form

Once dry, carefully remove the plaster from the box mold and pull the clay from the plaster. Brush off the remaining clay with a toothbrush. Now paint your bas relief. On the textural areas, also put glitter to bring out the texture even more distinctly. Let it dry. You can seal it with Mod Podge if you want to keep it.

This kind of sculpture focuses on actual texture. You can actually touch it and feel the bumpiness of the artwork.

😊 🟢 EXPLORATION: Grit

Cut fuzzy yarn into pieces of various lengths. Give each child a sheet of 40 grit sandpaper and let them use the yarn to make pictures on the sandpaper. The gritty texture of the sandpaper will hold the yarn in place. Have them try to make a fish, a flower, a tree, a house, and an ice cream cone. Then set them free to create whatever they want. They might even want to practice their spelling words or write their name with the yarn.

😊 🟢 🔵 EXPLORATION: Sculpture

To study form, you can look at a variety of sculptures in books, but it will be far more effective to take a trip to a museum to see them in person. Since form is 3 dimensional, it is most effectively seen that way.

Create your own sculptures too. You can use clay, play-doh, salt dough, or any other kind of dough available and practice making your own. You can either start with a block and carve away at it to create your form, or create smaller elements which you then attach and smooth together using a bit of water.

Low relief means the figures are raised slightly from the background, perhaps a few inches.

Bas relief figure, temple of Luxor, ancient Egypt.

Middle relief figures are raised slightly more. High relief figures are raised considerably from the background slab.

High relief on a building in Bishopsgate, London.

Coming up next . . .

Unit I-14
Ancient Africa
Africa – Bonding
African Tales

Ancient India – Grasslands – Elements – Texture & Form

My Ideas For This Unit:

Title: _____   Topic: _____

_____
_____
_____
_____
_____
_____
_____
_____

Title: _____   Topic: _____

_____
_____
_____
_____
_____
_____
_____
_____

Title: _____   Topic: _____

_____
_____
_____
_____
_____
_____
_____
_____

Ancient India – Grasslands – Elements – Texture & Form

My Ideas For This Unit:

Title: _____   Topic: _____

_____
_____
_____
_____
_____
_____
_____
_____
_____

Title: _____   Topic: _____

_____
_____
_____
_____
_____
_____
_____
_____
_____
_____

Title: _____   Topic: _____

_____
_____
_____
_____
_____
_____
_____
_____
_____

Buddha

Buddha means "enlightened one." Though destined to be brought up as a prince, Siddhartha left that life to meditate and discover truth. He sat under a tree for 49 days and then said he reached enlightenment. He then traveled from place to place and taught his beliefs to others. This was the beginning of Buddhism.

Layers of Learning

Ancient India: Unit 1-13

c. 3500 BC
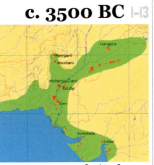
Farmers settle in the Indus valley

3120 BC

Mythical war of the Mahabharata

2500-1800 BC

Indus valley civilization at its height

c. 1500 BC

Aryan tribes from the northwest invade

1000 BC

The Rig-Veda are composed

876 BC
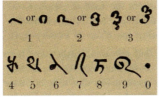
Hindus invent the concept of zero as a place holder

700 BC

Caste system begun

c. 560-480 BC

Siddhartha Gautama (Buddha) lives

500 BC
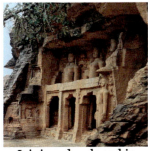
Jainism developed in Northern India

321 BC
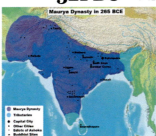
The Mauryan Empire begins

272-231 BC

Ashoka the Great is emperor

250 BC

First Buddhist cave temples are carved

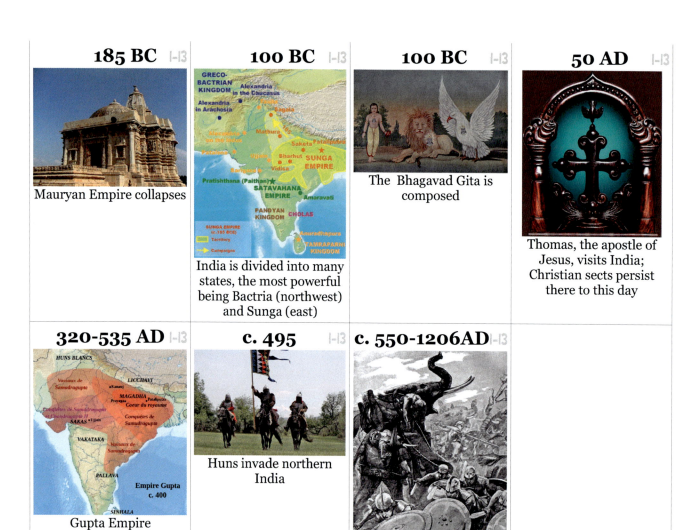

185 BC — Mauryan Empire collapses

100 BC — India is divided into many states, the most powerful being Bactria (northwest) and Sunga (east)

100 BC — The Bhagavad Gita is composed

50 AD — Thomas, the apostle of Jesus, visits India; Christian sects persist there to this day

320-535 AD — Gupta Empire

c. 495 — Huns invade northern India

c. 550-1206 AD — Dozens of small states vie for power in India

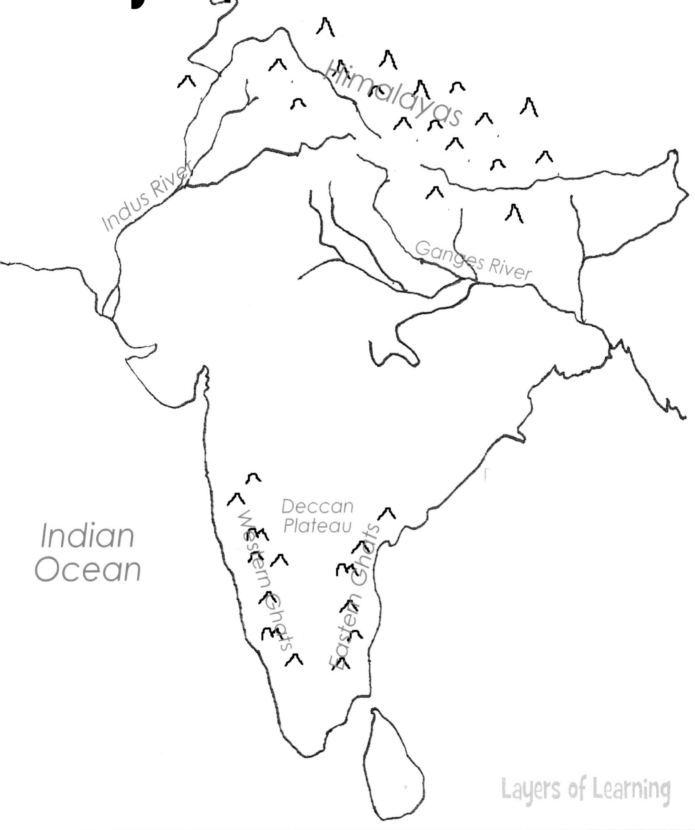

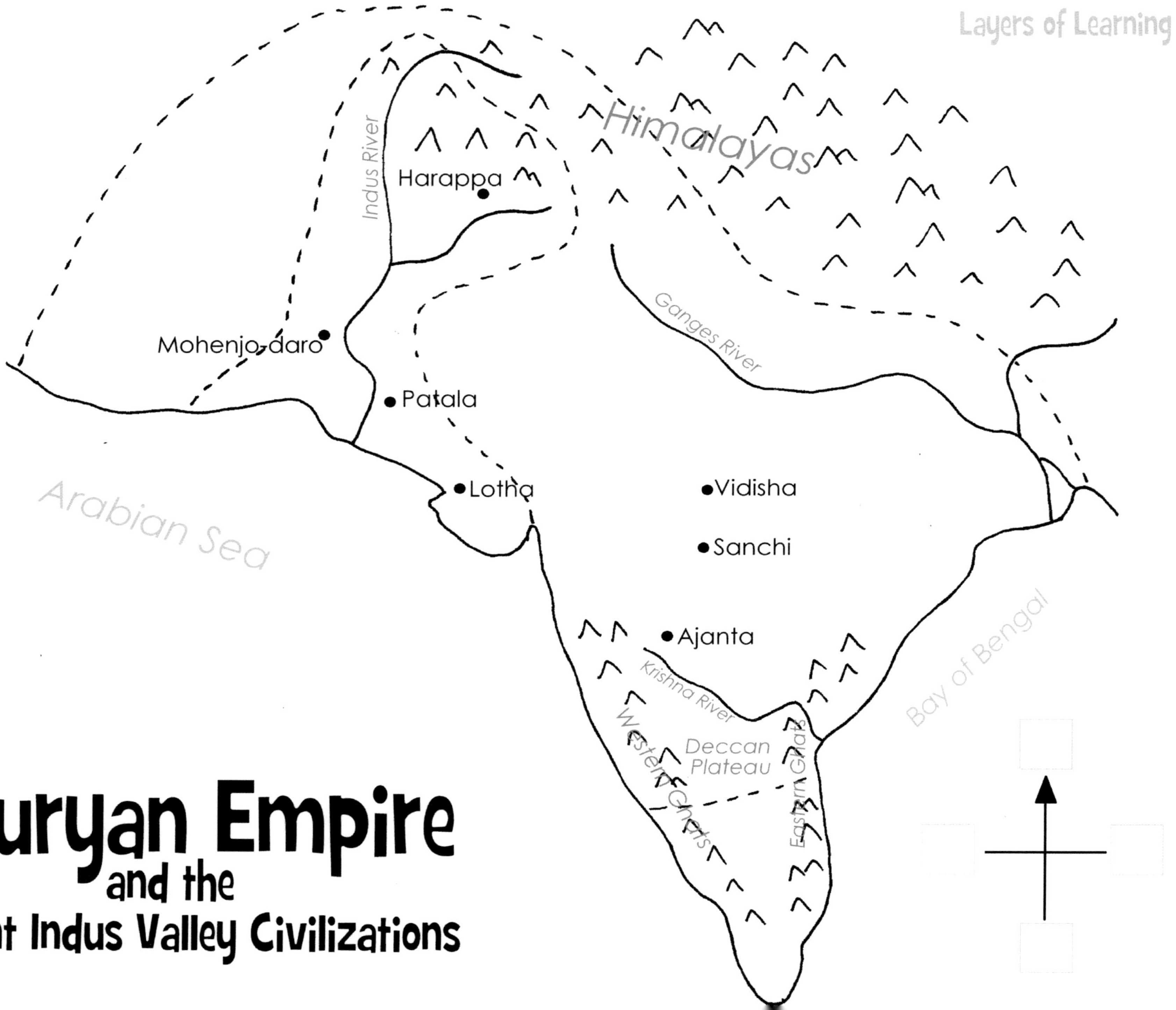

Mauryan Empire
and the Ancient Indus Valley Civilizations

Layers of Learning

- Mohenjo-daro
- Harappa
- Patala
- Lothal
- Vidisha
- Sanchi
- Ajanta

Himalayas
Indus River
Ganges River
Krishna River
Deccan Plateau
Western Ghats
Eastern Ghats
Arabian Sea
Bay of Bengal

Cast Into an Indian Caste

Learn each of the castes and color the pyramid. Outside of the pyramid you can add the pariahs, the untouchable members of society who were considered unclean. You may want to draw a person who belongs in each of the castes.

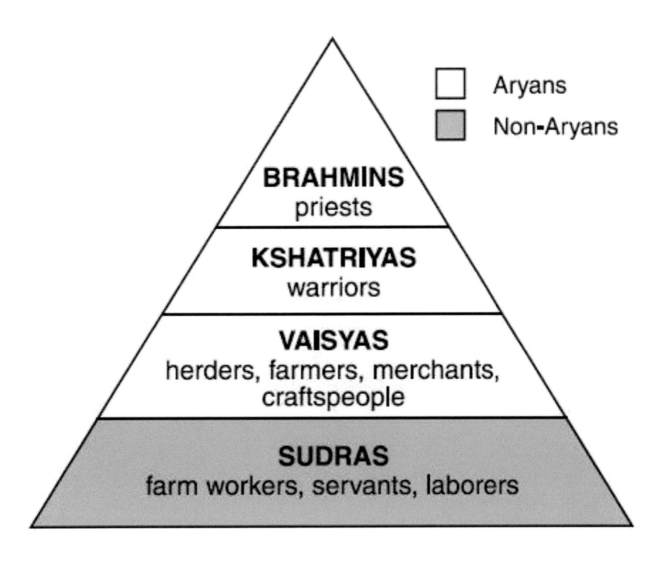

Grasslands of the World

Asia

Australia

Pacific Ocean

Indian Ocean

Arctic Ocean

Europe

Africa

Atlantic Ocean

North America

South America

Pacific Ocean

Layers of Learning

Grasslands

Grassland Game

Take turns rolling a single die. Proceed through the grasslands, but watch out for tornadoes, stampeeding bovines, and rough terrain. First one to the finish wins. Use small toys, coins, or buttons for markers.

Insects

There are many kinds of insects that live on the prairie. Locusts are one of the most prevalent. They eat grass and crops and can do lots of damage.

Burrowing

Some animals like the North Ameriocan Prairie Dog live in underground burrows. This keeps them safe from predators and gives them a home that is cool in the summer and warm in the winter.

Snakes

Rattlesnakes are one type of snake that lives in grasslands. They eat rodents and insects and can be dangerous to cattle and people.

Wildflowers

Wildflowers cover the plains. Echinacea is a purple flower that can be used as medicine also.

Periodic Table of the Elements

1 H Hydrogen 1.0																	2 He Helium 4.0
3 Li Lithium 6.9	4 Be Beryllium 9.0											5 B Boron 10.8	6 C Carbon 12.0	7 N Nitrogen 14.0	8 O Oxygen 16.0	9 F Fluorine 19.0	10 Ne Neon 20.2
11 Na Sodium 23.0	12 Mg Magnesium 24.3											13 Al Aluminum 27.0	14 Si Silicon 28.1	15 P Phosphorus 31.0	16 S Sulfur 32.1	17 Cl Chlorine 35.5	18 Ar Argon 40.0
19 K Potassium 39.1	20 Ca Calcium 40.1	21 Sc Scandium 45.0	22 Ti Titanium 47.9	23 V Vanadium 50.9	24 Cr Chromium 52.0	25 Mn Manganese 54.9	26 Fe Iron 55.9	27 Co Cobalt 58.9	28 Ni Nickel 58.7	29 Cu Copper 63.5	30 Zn Zinc 65.4	31 Ga Gallium 69.7	32 Ge Germanium 72.6	33 As Arsenic 74.9	34 Se Selenium 79.0	35 Br Bromine 79.9	36 Kr Krypton 83.8
37 Rb Rubidium 85.5	38 Sr Strontium 87.6	39 Y Yttrium 88.9	40 Zr Zirconium 91.2	41 Nb Niobium 92.9	42 Mo Molybdenum 95.9	43 Tc Technetium 99	44 Ru Ruthenium 101.0	45 Rh Rhodium 102.9	46 Pd Palladium 106.4	47 Ag Silver 107.9	48 Cd Cadmium 112.4	49 In Indium 114.8	50 Sn Tin 118.7	51 Sb Antimony 121.8	52 Te Tellurium 127.6	53 I Iodine 126.9	54 Xe Xenon 131.3
55 Cs Cesium 132.9	56 Ba Barium 137.3	Lanthanides 57-71	72 Hf Hafnium 178.5	73 Ta Tantalum 180.9	74 W Tungsten 183.9	75 Re Rhenium 186.2	76 Os Osmium 190.2	77 Ir Iridium 192.2	78 Pt Platinum 195.1	79 Au Gold 197.0	80 Hg Mercury 200.6	81 Tl Thallium 204.4	82 Pb Lead 207.2	83 Bi Bismuth 209.0	84 Po Polonium 210.0	85 At Astatine 211	86 Rn Radon 222.0
87 Fr Francium 223.0	88 Ra Radium 226.0	Actinides 89-103	104 Rf Rutherfordium 267	105 Db Dubnium 268	106 Sg Seaborgium 271	107 Bh Bohrium 272	108 Hs Hassium 270	109 Mt Meitnerium 276	110 Ds Darmstadtium 281	111 Rg Roentgenium 280	112 Cn Copernicium 285	113 Uut Ununtrium 284	114 Fl Flerovium 289	115 Uup Ununpentium 288	116 Lv Livermorium 293	117 Uus Ununseptium 294	118 Uuo Ununoctium 294

57 La Lanthanum 138.9	58 Ce Cerium 140.1	59 Pr Praseodymium 140.9	60 Nd Neodymium 144.2	61 Pm Promethium 145	62 Sm Samarium 150.4	63 Eu Europium 152.0	64 Gd Gadolinium 157.3	65 Tb Terbium 158.9	66 Dy Dysprosium 162.5	67 Ho Holmium 164.0	68 Er Erbium 167.3	69 Tm Thulium 168.9	70 Yb Ytterbium 173.0	71 Lu Lutetium 175.0
89 Ac Actinium 227.0	90 Th Thorium 232.0	91 Pa Protactinium 231.0	92 U Uranium 238.0	93 Np Neptunium 237	94 Pu Plutonium 242	95 Am Americium 243	96 Cm Curium 247	97 Bk Berkelium 247	98 Cf Californium 251	99 Es Einsteinium 254	100 Fm Fermium 253	101 Md Mendelevium 256	102 No Nobelium 254	103 Lr Lawrencium 257

Layers of Learning

Rare Earth Elements

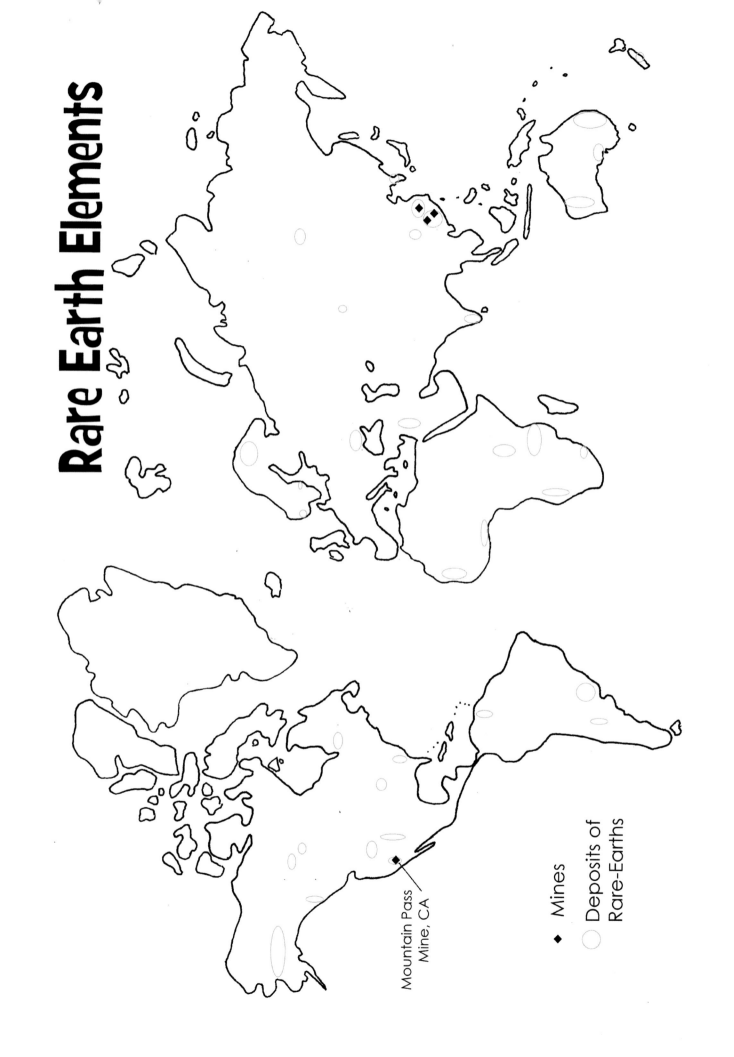

ABOUT THE AUTHORS

Karen & Michelle . . .
Mothers, sisters, teachers, women who are passionate
about educating kids.
We are dedicated to lifelong learning.

Karen, a mother of four, who has homeschooled her kids for more than eight years with her husband, Bob, has a bachelor's degree in child development with an emphasis in education. She lives in Utah where she gardens, teaches piano, and plays an excruciating number of board games with her kids. Karen is our resident Arts expert and English guru {most necessary as Michelle regularly and carelessly mangles the English language and occasionally steps over the bounds of polite society}.

Michelle and her husband, Cameron, homeschooling now for over a decade, teach their six boys on their ten acres in beautiful Idaho country. Michelle earned a bachelors in biology, making her the resident Science expert, though she is mocked by her friends for being the *Botanist with the Black Thumb of Death*. She also is the go-to for History and Government. She believes in staying up late, hot chocolate, and a no whining policy. We both pitch in on Geography, in case you were wondering, and are on a continual quest for knowledge.

*Visit our constantly updated blog for tons of free ideas,
free printables, and more cool stuff for sale:*
www.Layers-of-Learning.com

Made in the USA
Monee, IL
15 August 2020